KB076454

The Korean Center for Nonviolent Communication SM

Publisher:
The Korean Center for Nonviolent Communication
3F. Namyang BLDG. 23, Samseong-ro 95-gil,
Gangnam-gu, Seoul, South Korea

e-mail: krnvc@book.org

Graphic design:
Ivan Savić

Editor:
Nada Ignjatović Savić

Edition: fourth

Number of copies: 2000

Printed by:
South Korea

South Korea 2018.

Nada Ignjatović-Savić:

SMILE KEEPERS 1

Program for promoting self and social awareness development
psychological workshops for children 5-10 years of age

JOY OF GRATITUDE
for the first edition of the Smile keepers 1

I appreciate that UNICEF supported and financially helped the realization of the project called "Programs for supporting and promoting child development within war affected social context", i.e. "SMILE KEEPERS" or "The Guardians of the Smile". That way UNICEF also made it possible to publish this book. I am also grateful to all the psychologists, pedagogues and preschool teachers from kindergartens in Belgrade, Bar, Budva, Herceg Novi and Tivat for their excellent work and contribution in the realization of the psychological workshops this book consists of. Their suggestions and comments helped this book to get the shape in which it is now in front of the readers.
I would also like to express my gratitude to all collaborators who took part in making this book. Also, I am especially grateful to Prof. Ivan Ivić who introduced me into the beauty of the search after the more complete understanding of mental development of children. His remarks put on the suggested text of the book have encouraged me to keep on and make this book available to the world. Above all, from the bottom of my heart, I thank the children from the mentioned kindergartens who gave life to this program and made it be in harmony with its title.

SOME FACTS AND LOTS OF JOY
instead of the foreword to the second edition

Till the October 1993, when the first edition of this manual was published, the program of psychological workshops "Smile Keepers 1" has been conducted only in the kindergartens in 6 towns in Serbia and Montenegro. Since then till June 1995, when the second edition was published, we notice with joy the fact that the program has been spread in 44 places: Aleksinac, Aranđelovac, Banja Koviljača, Bar, Beograd, Bijela, Budva, Bujanovac, Valjevo, Vranje, Vranjska banja, Gornji Milanovac, Zrenjanin, Jabuka, Jagodina, Kačarevo, Kikinda, Knjaževac, Kotor, Kragujevac, Kruševac, Lazarevac, Lajkovac, Loznica, Leskovac, Ljubovija, Mionica, Negotin, Niš, Novi Sad, Obrenovac, Pančevo, Paraćin, Pirot, Petrovac na moru, Petrovac na Mlavi, Požarevac, Smederevo, Sremska Kamenica, Sopot, Tivat, Užice, Herceg Novi. Apart from kindergartens, the program has been accepted by schools and children's homes. 16000 of preschool and elementary school children and 1200 of adults who are taking care of them are involved until now in the vibrant network of smile keepers. Thousand reasons for joy!
The results of the analysis of the effects of the program are showing significant positive changes in the behavior of children. In short, according

to the assessment of the teachers, children that underwent the program become more open, more free in expressing their feelings, more sensitive to the others, more attentive and persistent in their work, more sociable, imaginative, curious, autonomous and self confident than before. There were also positive changes noticed on the level of the group/class – mutual confidence and cooperation increased.

Teachers are emphasizing that these workshops were for them a very precious opportunity to get to know the soul of each child. The children are also emphasizing that it was very important for them to express their inner world in the presence of teachers and to get their support and understanding. For the author of this program, it was especially pleasant to see that, according to the evaluation of both children and teachers, among the favorite workshops were those dealing with the most delicate psychological topics: feelings of anger, fear, sadness and conflicts... This is indeed confirming once more that the program is in tune with the needs of children.

The reason for joy is also the fact that the most popular among children was the workshop on love. Children know what is most important in life!

The second edition is not essentially different from the first one. Some necessary corrections in the graphic design of the book were made, and that's all.

EDITION "SMILE KEEPERS 1", 2007

13 years have passed since the second edition of this manual was published. Many reasons for joy and celebration accumulated in that period.

The teachers appreciate the 'Smile Keepers 1' program, so that new groups of children are introduced to it continuously. The author no longer has a clear overview of how many children were reached, though the number is clearly more than one hundred thousand. About 1200 teachers per year receive training for the Smile Keepers program.

Since 2001, this program has been acknowledged as an integral part of the Civic (Democratic citizenship) Education for the first grade of Elementary school. The Ministry of Education of Serbia has organized extensive trainings for interested teachers, and this program is now present in almost all schools in Serbia. The program underwent external evaluation performed by UNESCO's and UNICEF's international experts, and was positively assessed.

2004 - This program was included in the Catalogue of programs accredited by the Ministry of Education of Serbia, and recommended as component of professional training for teachers.

2003-2004 - In collaboration with the educative program team of national TV, the author created a Smile Keepers TV serial, 33 workshop-episodes with the same group of children, and was very well received by child audiences. This year the second showing of TV Smile Keepers will be aired in the school program of national TV.

2006 - In collaboration with MPPP - Methodic Center for Psycho pedagogic assistance in Education in Poland, the author has trained the team of trainers to educate teachers in Poland to conduct Smile Keepers programs with children. The programs are then translated to polish.

2006 - Several groups of teachers from Germany, Switzerland, Belgium, France and Luxembourg expressed interest in applying this program in their schools. That was the reason for this edition.

This edition has been extended into two workshops aiming at informing children's parents about the program and its effects (workshop 1 and 32), the evaluative workshop (31.), and 7 new workshops on the themes the teachers reported as important for the children (9, 17, 18, 25, 26, 29, 30).

INTRODUCTION

"There are rivers in each of us
Meeting under this very same bridge,
That's why our happiness and sadness
Are so differently of the same kind."

Miroslav Antić
"This Is How I Imagine Heaven"

This book is directed at the adults who are ready to enjoy, together with children, the beauty of the discovery of how we are different, yet are the same. The book was conceived over a long period of time, but was written in just a couple of days. Year after year new parts have been added, experiences of others were incorporated, as well as my own efforts to transform theoretical theses on *the formative role of social interaction upon the mental development of children*' into a series of concrete, practical activities consisting of growth nurturing exchanges between adults and children. The urgent and strong need to protect the development of children deprived by the war was what led to crystallizing all the accumulated experience into the shape it has now, here in front of you.

"SMILE KEEPERS I" hopefully presents the first in a series of printed products with the same title. The program is offered at the Institute of Psychology and, sponsored by UNICEF, is being applied in kindergartens and schools in Serbia and Montenegro since February 1993. The Project consists of two parts: one directed by Vesna Ognjenovic, and the other one by the author of this book. Both of them consist of special psychological workshop programs for educating grown up Smile Keepers - preschool, elementary and high school teachers, psychologists, pedagogues as well as programs of stimulation of self and social awareness development for children of different ages - from preschool to adolescent years. Each of these programs might become the next "SMILE KEEPERS" book. Moreover, during the phase of the realization of the Project several thousands of children's creations have been collected. A selected sample of children's drawings, which decorate the first edition of this manual, can only give a slight insight into the richness, value and variety of these creations from children's hands and minds. Out of that treasury several interesting books could be written to testify of the mental universe of children who live in today's world.

The book in front of you is a revised and expanded version of a handbook originally created for preschool teachers who participated in the project. All of them attended educative workshops before starting to work with children. These workshops were aimed to develop sensitivity to the problems workshop leaders might encounter, to strengthen their educative competence, their meta-educative attitude or "deliberate spontaneity" in relation to children. This 'learning through experience' cannot be replaced by merely reading instructions on 'how to lead workshops', no matter how well and detailed they are written. The benefit of experiential learning lies not only in the cognitive domain, but also in the joy that's being released, and spreads almost contagiously among participants during workshops. And there is the author's dilemma concerning publishing this manual: on one hand, there is a wish to make the program which has such positive effects available to as many potential users as possible, and, on the other hand, there is doubt that somebody who has not had a direct, personal experience with these kinds of workshops, might not be able to feel and transfer all of the beauty of getting to know each other in this way to the children.

In other words, the question is: could you become a Smile Keeper just following the static script? It is obvious that the hope that it is possible has won over the doubt.

The best criterion of success for the program and for the leader is the children's behavior. If they wait for the workshop to begin curiously and cheerfully, if their drawings and other responses bear the stamps of their own uniqueness, if they listen to each other with attention and are busy exploring themselves and others - you know that the Smile Keeper is with them.

THEORETICAL STANDPOINT

The theoretic basis of this program is a combination of interactivist and constructivist approach to the nature of human development, relying on Vygotskian's theory of development and M. B. Rosenberg's Model of Nonviolent Communication.

We consider the following thesis to be relevant for the program:

A child's experience of the world, and of him or herself in that world, is mediated by the adults.
- adults organize the environment and sharing in such a way that a child can understand and accept it;
- adults help the children to face relevant, specifically chosen stimuli which lead them to higher developmental stages but protect them from experiences hard to cope with at this age;

• Adults encourage all spontaneous attempts a child makes to explore and learn about him/herself and the world, and tries to make it a pleasant, positive experience for children.

Children are active participants in the interaction.
• a child chooses, rearranges and keeps for himself just what is in accordance with his developmental needs and powers;
• a path from outer to inner space, from exchange to creating an inner, private, psychological world leads through play in which a child in his/hers special way puts things together he/she has collected through these exchanges with others.

The goal of this psychological workshops program is to help children, through interactions in a playful context, to build emotional stability, to develop optimal strategies to overcome unpleasant mental states, conflicts, to promote skills of self-expression and communication, to strengthen self-confidence and confidence in others, and to enrich their learning about themselves and others.

PRINCIPLES OF APPROACH

• No ready-made solutions are offered, nor are 'right answers' required of the children. The focus lies on the **process** of discovery, on learning, and not on the outcome. The learning happens through **play**.

• **Adults and children equally take an active part in that process.** Of course, this doesn't mean that children know as much as adults. The specific trait of a child - adult relationship lies right there in its **asymmetry:** adults know a lot more about themselves, the world and about children. But, in order to be able to give the necessary and well-timed stimulation to each child, an adult needs to know how to listen with special attention and sensitivity, and to be open to take and give importance to what the children communicate. The poet Duško Radović beautifully describes these qualities with the term "**respected children**".

• Adults organize activities in such a way that the children feel the need and desire to share **among themselves, and not only with adults**.

• Adults **give directions (working in the zone of proximal development)** without forcing anything, they flexibly move between symmetric and asymmetric position, between support and stimulation.

- Adults nurture a **positive** approach: they comment and direct attention to what is valuable and unique in every child, and articulate it in a **concrete** way ("I like that you did it that way") and not generally ("You are good").

- Adults create an **atmosphere of confidence** and acceptance, **without judgments or criticism**.

- Adults sensitively respond to the children's emotional reactions: children feel safer in an environment where **their feelings are cared for,** and where they can freely express all their moods.

- Adults **respect outbursts of negative feelings**: allowing time for them to express (fear, anger, frustrations...), don't interrupt with questions, nor suffocate them ("Don't cry, it is nothing."). They help the child to differentiate what he/she is feeling and why by checking: "Are you sad because you want company, are you angry because you want to choose what you want to do?" They support and encourage the children to use their energy constructively without hurting themselves or others.

- They show that they appreciate, and are happy when the children overcome difficulties. They teach the children how to enjoy in their achievements and how to **express that they are proud and satisfied with themselves**.

- Adults are at all times aware of the fact that **their own behavior as a model affects** the behavior of the children. Children imitate and mold their behavior in accordance to what they observe in adults.

- **Adults nurture tolerance**, understanding and cooperation, meaning they themselves act in a calm way, full of understanding, without aggression.

- Adults support **uniqueness** and stress the fact that each of us is special and unique, and that differences make us richer. The most important task in an education is to help children to develop self-esteem, to become self-confident, and aware that by giving to others and taking from others their lives becomes enriched.

In the core of the program are activities asking for symbolic expression (drawing, pantomime, symbolic play, drama play) and sharing around the circle. In that way the children are able to become aware of their inner experiences.
Relaxation exercises and motoric games help the children to get rid of tension, and to create a good mood in a group.

WHAT IS IMPORTANT
for workshop leaders to remember

1. To create a **pleasant atmosphere** where the children feel safe and re-lax-ed.
2. **Not to raise the voice**. At the beginning make a deal with the children about the "Silence!" or "Attention!" signs (it could be a drawing, or a sound signal, anything, as long it is presented from the heart and with smile).
3. **To explain to the children some workshop rules**:
   a) They are going to sit in a circle like the Knights of the Round Table, so they can see each other, listen to each other, and learn from each other;
   NOTE: when children draw, or play roles etc, they are free to move around;
   b) everyone will say or do something when their turn comes;
   c) it is important that they look at, and listen to others, because they are going to learn a lot from that, and this way will become aware that there are similarities and differences between them;
   d) there are no right answers; it is important that they say what they really feel and think;
   NOTE: it could be a problem that the children want to know how "good" they are in certain activities and try to guess what the adults expect from them. It should be stressed that everything that is genuinely theirs is welcomed;
   f) Sometimes they can say: "Pass", if they don't know what to say or do;
   NOTE: resistance is to be respected but it also should be noted when and who refuses to share something. Pay attention to reserved (silent) children and do not insist on their speaking – it is ok to let them skip sharing around the circle now and then;
   If there are children who often interrupt and disturb group work, they could be kindly reminded of the rule: "That is interesting, but wait for your turn to come". If that doesn't help, create a circle of sharing about "**how we feel when somebody interrupts**" and one "**about reasons which sometimes keep us from listening to others**."
4. If a group refuses to work - see what the problem is, adjust the script, play some games that are interesting to them.
5. It is optimal that two people lead the workshops – a **workshop-leader** who follows the script and stimulates the exchanges in the group and an **assistant** who writes down everything the children say, from the first to the closing circle (e.g., in the circle of names, and what I like: Mary- likes to swim, Peter- likes to eat, etc.).
   The written report needs to contain following data:
   - Time, place, participants;

- Name of the leader;
- All activities done in order they were done, and all responses of the children.
6. The optimal number of children-participants is from 10-15. You can work with a group up to 20 children, but then attention span and motivation to share decline. Some children cannot wait their turn to come and, what is also important; cannot follow that much individual expression with attention. If the group is big, it would be better to divide it into two groups, where more intensive sharing can happen.
7. Rhythm of work: 1-2 workshops a week are optimal. Then a leader has enough time to *settle impressions* on every child and children can build on the experience they made during the sharing through spontaneous symbolic play.
8. Each workshop should last about one hour. Of course, it depends on the number of participants and on the level of their involvement in activities.
9. After each workshop, workshop leaders are supposed to create the symbol/drawing of that workshop together with the children and put it up on the panel. This will remind them of what they have passed.

WHAT ELSE IS IMPORTANT TO KNOW

This program is made for children from 5 to 10 years old. So, it can be applied with elementary school children, but for children under the age of five, a lot of requests would be too complex. Some changes in the scripts would have to be made according to the responses of the children (the basic principle of the program is that the adults align themselves to the children's level of understanding.) But, doing that, the fact should be stressed that neither the sequence of workshops, nor the sequence of activities in each workshop is random. Each of these workshops follows this pattern: activity that leads to problem analysis (conflict, unpleasant emotional state, etc.) and then activity through which a child can find a constructive way out of that state. So, whatever the reason, the workshop should not be finished before the children were given an opportunity to learn how to overcome the things that bother them. At the same time, workshops are put in that order so children can gradually face unpleasant and painful topics and in the closing workshops the stress is on positive feelings and appreciation.

Dealing with suffering, difficult experiences and serious problems some children carry within them could frighten and upset the teacher. In that case, one should without hesitation share one's worries and ask for advice from a school psychologist.

WORKSHOP No. 1

THE INTRODUCTORY MEETING OF STUDENTS, THEIR PARENTS AND WORKSHOP LEADER(S)

THE WORKSHOP SCHEMA

1. Presentation of the **basic features** of the method of work

2. Parents say their names and one thing they like about themselves

3. Children say their names and one thing they like about themselves

4. What parents remember as pleasant/unpleasant from their school-days

5. What children find pleasant/unpleasant about school

6. Children propose what could be done to make school more pleasant for them

7. Overview of the Smile Keepers Program

8. Questions about the program

9. A **stretching game**

THE INTRODUCTORY MEETING OF STUDENTS, THEIR PARENTS AND WORKSHOP LEADER(S)

This scenario is just a suggestion. The workshop leader could design this part in a way they like. It is only important that the children and parents get insight into WHAT the program is about and HOW it will be done.

1. Workshop leader (WL) is asking children and parents to sit in two semi circles, facing each other. After greeting them, WL briefly presents the **basic features** of the method of the workshop (learning as pleasant, playful activity of sharing, getting to know themselves and others through sharing around the circle, etc.)

2. WL asks parents to say their name and one thing they like about themselves (if they are hesitant to start encourage them by saying something like: it is important for all of us to be aware of our qualities and to feel free to speak about that). **Sharing around the circle of parents**.

3. WL asks children to say their name and one thing they like about themselves. **Sharing around the circle of children**.

4. WL asks parents to remember something from their first schooldays, which was pleasant/unpleasant for them. **Sharing around the circle of parents**.

5. WL asks children to say what they find pleasant/unpleasant about going to school. **Sharing around the circle of children**.

6. WL asks children to propose what could be done to make them feel more pleasant in the school **(Sharing, who wants to)**.

7. WL briefly presents the Smile Keepers Program.

8. WL invites parents and children to ask questions about the program.

9. **Stretching game**: all participants (parents and children) are standing so that they can have enough space to move hands up and down. WL is asking them to touch their toes with their fingers (or if they cannot reach their toes, to touch their legs where they can reach). Then WL starts to count slowly from 1 to 10 and participants are supposed to raise their hands up, so that at 10 they are above their heads. They also need to remember the position of the hands for each count from 1 to 10.

Than the game starts - WL is randomly saying the numbers, and participants need to put their hands in the position corresponding to that number.

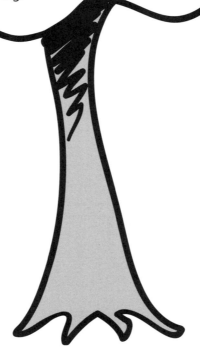

WORKSHOP No. 2

SELF AWARENESS (1)

THE WORKSHOP SHEMA

1. **Circle of names:** clap your hands and say your name

2. **Do you like your name?**

3. **What name would you like to have? Why?**

4. **Say what you like to do**

5. **Make a self-portrait**

6. **Sharing around the circle:** Show and describe what you have drawn

THE GOAL of the workshop:
- to make children aware of themselves, their specific traits, differences and similarities to stimulate imagination;
- To stimulate sharing.

WORKSHOP No. 2

SELF AWARENESS (1)

1. **Circle of names:** *clap your hands and say your name, one by one around the circle.*

2. **Do you like your name?** *Tap your knees if you like it, wave with your finger if you do not like it.*

3. *If you could choose, which name would you give to yourself?* **What name would you like to have?** *Why?*

4. *Say something* **you enjoy doing** *(I like to....)*

5. *Draw yourself on this paper (A4 sheet):* **make your self-portrait.** *Draw so it can be recognized that it is you. When they finish drawing, say: And now, in a cloud (remind them of clouds in cartoons where it says what a character thinks)* **show how you feel today,** *what mood you are in. Choose colors, which express what you feel. If your mood has changed since this morning, show it with different colors. When they all finished this task:*

6. **Sharing around the circle:** *Show us and describe what you have drawn.* Praise each child, but without judging the quality of the drawings. It could be done in this way: *"There it really can be seen what is important to you",* and *"How all the drawings are different and beautiful in their own way".*

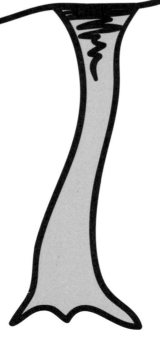

WORKSHOP No. 3

SELF AWARENESS (2)

THE WORKSHOP SHEMA

1. **Transformation game**: sharing around the circle

2. **Name something you can do**, **you are satisfied with**, sharing around the circle

3. **What do you like about yourself?** Sharing around the circle

4. **Make your own badge**

5. **present your badge to everyone in the group**

THE GOAL of the workshop:
- to make children aware of themselves, their characteristics and the differences and similarities between them;
- to stimulate imagination;
- to stimulate sharing.

SELF AWARENESS (2)

1. **Transformation game:** *Think: if you were an animal, which animal would you like to be?* (pause) *Why? What do you like about that animal?* (pause) Sharing around the circle:" I would like to be X because...."

2. ***Name something you can do, where you are satisfied with the way you do it?*** (For ex, to tell jokes, to play football, etc.) What the child appreciates about himself. Sharing around the circle.

3. ***What do you like about yourself?*** Sharing around the circle: "I like..."

4. ***Make your own badge:*** *it should contain your name and something that characterizes you -- your personal sign, drawing, or shape of your choosing.* (Encourage them to use colors and all available material in their own way, to find their own shape, size, color, their own symbol...) (to put the badges on, use safety pins or tape).

5. ***Walk around with your badge on.*** *In* your own way present yourself to everyone in the group and go to look at the other's badges.

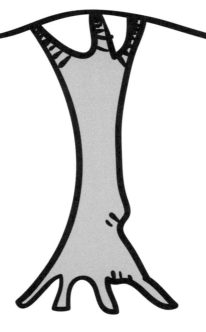

WORKSHOP No. 4

TIME TRAVEL (SELF-CONTINUITY)

THE WORKSHOP SCHEMA

1. **Names circle:** alternately quiet and loud

2. **Time travel**

3. **Make your own comic**

4. **WL comment**

5. **Pleasant memories postures**

6. **Confidence exercise: walk in pairs**

THE GOAL of the workshop:
- to make the children aware of the characteristics, differences and similarities they share;
- to notice what are important (pleasant and unpleasant) points in life;
- to activate pleasant memories;
- to stimulate positive feelings and a positive attitude towards oneself and others.

TIME TRAVEL (SELF-CONTINUITY)

1. **Names circle:** they say their names alternately quiet and loud.

2. ***Let's climb into a time machine*** (explain that it is a special device that can travel across time). *Prepare yourself for an imaginary journey. Close your eyes! We travel across time and pretend that we take pictures with a camera. We go back to the past. Think of something that happened to you from **your birthday** until now. Remember what you have experienced, what was pleasant, what was not pleasant, when were you especially happy, when did you cry. You need to take several photos. On these photos, you can also put those who were with you then...* (After a couple of minutes) *Open your eyes.*

3. **Make your own comic:** *Draw your experiences. Make a few drawings as if you were making a comic book. For example: the first picture could be your birthday celebration. Draw on it: who was with you, where were you... Then the next picture can present something else that happened to you, e.g., when you were crying... Then something pleasant on the next...* (Give them paper-tape 12 cm x 60cm and show them how to make the cartoon). When they finish drawing: *Now put a red circle on the pictures on which you were happy. Put a blue circle on those pictures on which you were sad (if there are any of those).* **Sharing around the circle**: everyone shows their drawing and talks about it.

4. **Pleasant memories:** *We all sometimes forget what it feels like to be joyful. Let us now remember how it felt when we were happy. When I give you this sign* (e.g., clapping hands) *everybody who sits here* (show exactly which children you mean, app. half of the group) *stand up and take a posture of joy. Faces and bodies should express joy. Stay that way until I clap my hands again. But do not move; keep that pose like on this photo* (show them a "frozen" posture). *The rest of us will be the audience. Then the 'audience' will*

make postures of joy. (Let the children pose for 10-15 sec, then point to the other half of the group to do the same).

5. **Confidence exercise:** *walk in pairs. Let us loosen ourselves a little! Since we have been sitting for a long time, we need some movement. But it would be more interesting if we did it in this way: let's get into pairs of "A" and "B". "A"s will close their eyes and "B"s will put their hands on "A"s shoulder and lead him/her around the room, wherever "B" wants to, but in silence. Try to make the walk pleasant and interesting for the person you lead, (be careful not to bump into others or hit something). It will be more interesting to play the game in silence. Let your hands speak. After a while* (about 3 min.) *when I give you a sign, you will change roles.*
NOTE: If they ask how they are supposed to lead without words, answer: *"Well, think of a way you could show just with your hand: go, turn, stop, etc."*
Sharing in the group: How did they feel playing both roles? What was more pleasant? They all now sit in a circle and tell about their walk, did they know where they were and were they confident in their leading-partners.

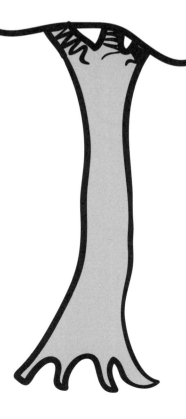

WORKSHOP No. 5

MY PLACE OF RELAXATION

THE WORKSHOP SCHEMA

1. **Walking on an imaginary surface**

2. **Relaxation and guided fantasy exercises**

3. **Drawing a place of relaxation: sharing around the circle**

4. **Confidence exercise:** rocking

THE GOAL of the workshop:
- to teach children how to relax;
- to stimulate imagination and help them create a place of relaxation;
- to stimulate sharing and mutual confidence.

MY PLACE OF RELAXATION

1. **Walking on the imaginary surface:** *"Let us pretend that there is glue on the floor or we jump from one imaginary stone to another, or we pretend to walk across snow, through the woods, desert..."*

2. **Relaxation exercise and guided fantasy:** *"And now, since we became tired of this walking, let's lie or sit down. But we are not going to sleep. We are going to keep walking in our imagination..."*
   NOTE: Before this exercise you need to explain to the children that they should keep their eyes closed and that they are going to do an exercise of relaxation and imagination. If a child opens the eyes before the end of the exercise, smile and support him/her nonverbally. Let him/her stay with the eyes open but in silence. Everyone should lie on the floor, or sit in a comfortable position with their eyes closed. The leader speaks slowly, and makes a lot of pauses in order to give the children time for the experience.

   a. Relaxation: *Breathe rhythmically, relax your legs and hands, feel that your head is relaxed, and your neck, and slowly try to find the most comfortable position. Close your eyes. I will take you on an imaginary journey. Now take a couple of very deep breaths. OK. Your eyes are closed and while I am talking, you imagine that you are going to an especially lovely place...* Pause.

   b. Guided fantasy: *Imagine that you are somewhere in the country side. You move slowly on a soft, pleasant surface. Choose your own way of moving, you can walk, or run, or roll... however you like. Keep your eyes closed.* Pause. *Go to a place where you know you will feel good. It can be a place from your dreams, or a place you have already been to. We slowly start to go there. Hear the sounds at that place, all the sounds you like. It could be the wind, the rain, a bird singing, water... whatever lets you feel good.* Pause. *See the colors and the light. The colors are very pleasant. You can feel how they relax* *you. You move and feel the easy breeze that touches your face, hands, and all of your body as it caresses you. And then you feel other things touching you as well. It could be the rain, snow, sunshine... whatever feels good to you.* Pause. *Now you smell the ground, and the plants. Now all the smells caress you. Breathe slowly and deeply and feel how relaxed you are.* Pause. *You are still moving through country side, you move slowly, deeply relaxed, and everything feels very nice.* Pause. *Slowly you arrive at your place of relaxation. Everything that makes you feel calm and satisfied will appear here around you the instant you wish for it.* Pause. *Add to that place all kinds of things that make you feel good. Here you are safe and completely relaxed; this is your place of relaxation.* Pause. *Look around and see where you are, what is there, who is there? Are there any people you know? Are there any animals? Is there anybody? How do you feel? Remember everything: colors... light... shapes... sounds... touches... smells...* Pause. *Now slowly prepare yourself for coming back. When you are ready, open your eyes and here you are again in this room. If somebody wants to get up and stretch their legs and arms – go ahead.* (Relaxation and guided fantasy all together last about 10 min.)

3. **Drawing a place of relaxation:** *Now make a drawing of your place of relaxation. With lines, shapes and colors show where you were, how you felt, what you saw and experienced. Put that experience on the paper. It is not important how you draw, what is important is that it means something to you.* (When they finish with the drawing) *Give a title to that place.* (Stimulate them to find their own titles for their places, e.g. "Anna's beach" or "Peter's valley").
Sharing around the circle: What is their place of relaxation? Where were they? How did they feel? At what point were they the most relaxed? What made them feel that way? What is the title of the place of relaxation and why?

4. **Confidence exercise:** rocking. They play this game in groups of 3. Two of them are standing face to face, the third stands in the middle. The two rock the one in the middle gently between them. The third should close his eyes and let them rock him. They push him gently, holding him by the shoulders. At the beginning they are very close together. Very slowly they can widen the distance (staying in the zone of gentle and safe rocking). (5-6 min.)

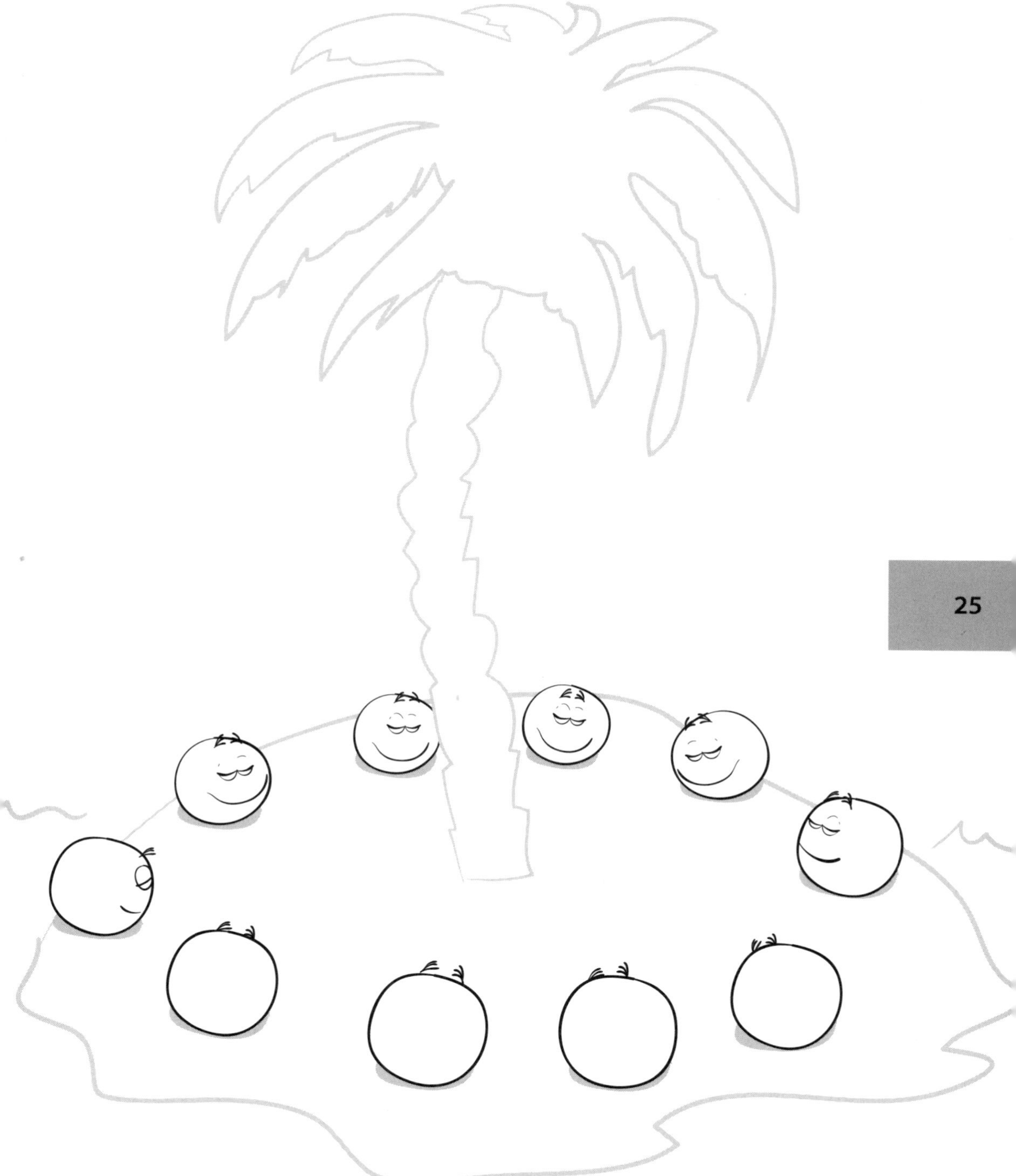

WORKSHOP No. 6

WHAT WORRIES ME

THE WORKSHOP SCHEMA

1. **Circle of names:** making gestures, others repeat

2. **My circle of worries: Drawing.** Sharing around the circle: impressions, the biggest worry

3. **What can you do to make yourself feel good**? Sharing around the circle.

4. **What are their helpers, what do they do?** Sharing around the circle.

5. **Relaxation exercises**: head-goes-around, get off my back, massaging necks and backs in a circle

THE GOAL of the workshop
- to stimulate a proactive attitude;
- to stimulate imagination and creativity;
- to teach the children a technique to release tension.

WHAT WORRIES ME

1. **Circle of names:** one child stands up, says her/his name, and makes a gesture (e.g.: "Marina" and spreads her arms or jumps on one foot.). All others then stand up and repeat her gesture and so on.

2. **My circle of worries:** Children get sheets of paper (A4) with a big circle already on it - children draw in that circle the things that worry them the most, the problems they think about.
   Sharing around the circle: Their impressions: *Was it difficult for you to draw this, what was difficult? What is your greatest worry?*

3. *What can we do to stop the worries that bother us? How can you make your day more beautiful? What can you do to make yourself feel good?* **Sharing around the circle.**

4. *What to do with worries that last more than a day? We can **create a helper** to deal with them. Now you surely wonder how. Well, this way: Close your eyes, relax and think of a creature or a thing that would help you to annul, clean out of your head things that worry you. It can be a creature from a fairy tale or a magic eraser or something your imagination will come up with. (In-spire them to look for funny, creative solution of their own.) Now each time that worry shows up, all you have to do is to turn that helper on -- think of a way, how to do that! Use your imagination.* Sharing around the circle: **what are their helpers, how do they turn them on.**

5. *We will do some exercises to loosen ourselves a little:*
   • **The first exercise: head-goes-around**. *Move your heads slowly to the left, backwards, to the right, back to the front; then repeat it the other way round, keeping your eyes closed. Imagine that your head is as light as a balloon. Repeat the exercise with eyes open, your eyes follow where your head is moving, without focusing them.*

- **The second exercise: get off my back**. *Stand upright with your feet apart and parallel, knees relaxed, relax your belly, bottom and shoulders, and let your arms hang. Breathe evenly and relax your jaws. Lift your elbows to the height of your shoulders, spread your arms and then pull them back with a sudden and strong move, shouting: "Get off my back!" Repeat the exercise several times; express your mood with your voice.* (demonstrate it)

Closing activity: Standing in a circle, everybody massages the person in front of them, and gets a massage from the one behind him.

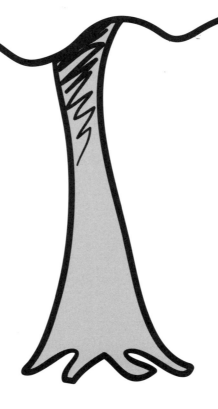

WORKSHOP No. 7

EXPRESSING FEELINGS

THE WORKSHOP SCHEMA

1. **Moving around the space** expressing a feeling

2. Body talk

3. **Circle of feelings:** Sharing around circle

4. **How does that circle change inside and why?** Sharing around circle

5. WL comment

THE GOAL of the workshop:
- to stimulate awareness and expression of feelings.

EXPRESSING FEELINGS

1. **Moving around the space:** All participants stand in a circle. The leader says: *When I give you a sign, you start walking around the room. Think now of a path you walk down. Then imagine that you are tired. How would you walk if you were tired? Ok, now start: tired...* (30 sec.) *And now as if you were angry...* (30 sec.) *And now scared...* (30 sec.) *Sad...* (30 sec.) *And now in a funny way...* (30 sec.) *And now joyfully ...* (30 sec.)
NOTE: Pay attention to nonverbal signs of anxiety: if children keep stiff while moving, if they keep their hands clenched, if they scratch themselves, or suck their fingers.

After they sit back in a circle:

2. **Body talk:** *What does our body do when we are tired? In what way does your body tell you that it is tired? When I give you a sign, show it with all of your body. Now let just your hands show that they are tired. Now show that you are tired just by your voice.* Repeat these questions in connection with the experiences of anger, fear, sadness, happiness.

3. **Circle of feelings:** *Now try to imagine that all the feelings, all the emotions you had for the last few days, are in a circle. How much space, which color and place would each of them take up? Express that on the paper, using lines, colors and shapes that express what you feel. How big and which color is your joy, fear, sadness, anger, love, jealousy? Use a different color for each feeling.*
Sharing around the circle: What do they have in their circles of feelings?

4. **How does that circle change inside?** *How do emotions change: suddenly, gradually? What does it depend on? For example – now you are sad, and now happy. Or you are happy and than a little bit less happy and then sad...* Sharing: they talk about how their moods change and what that depends on.
WL COMMENT: our feelings are giving us signs, which show if what we want or need is fulfilled or not. For example, when you need tenderness and mum or dad is caressing you: you are satisfied; if you miss being caressed you are sad.

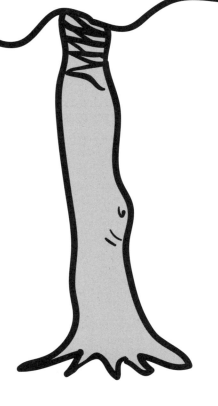

WORKSHOP No. 8

COMMUNICATING FEELINGS

THE WORKSHOP SCHEMA

1. **Exercises in pairs: mirror of emotions**

2. **WL comment**

3. **Communicating with the back of the body. Sharing around circle**

4. **Guessing feeling game**

5. **Confidence exercise in pairs: seesaw**

THE GOAL of the workshop:
- to stimulate observing and expressing feelings;
- To stimulate sharing.

COMMUNICATING FEELINGS

1. **Exercises in pairs: mirror of emotions**. They make pairs "A" and "B". When the leader gives a sign "A" changes facial expressions, expressing different emotions. "B" imitates "A" simultaneously, as if "B" were "A"'s reflection in the mirror. After 2 - 3 minutes, roles change. Stress that they should not use their hands or anything else except their faces!
   Sharing in a group: How did they feel in both roles, what did they like, what didn't they like? What was more difficult, to express or to mirror?

2. **WL COMMENT**: This exercise is not only a good gymnastic for the face, but also helps us to become more aware of how many muscles take part in our emotions, how many expressions our face can produce and what wealth that is.

3. **Communicating with the back of your body:** Pairs are sitting back to back, touching each other with the whole surface of the back. (Demonstrate it). When a sign is given, "A" is to communicate an emotion to "B" only by using his back. When the transmission is over, "A" says: "Over". You could offer them to choose one of the following 4 feelings: JOY, SADNESS, ANGER, and FEAR. "A" gets to choose what and how to express. When they finished with one turn, they change roles. It would be good if each player expresses at least 4 different feelings.
   Sharing in the circle: did they succeed to recognize feelings? How did they feel playing?

4. **Guessing feelings game:** A child thinks of something that happened to him and demonstrates the feeling with facial expressions and body movements. The rest of the group guesses what the feeling is. The child that guesses correctly gets to go next.

5. **Confidence exercise in pairs: seesaw**. Pairs stand holding each other by the wrists and simultaneously squat and stand up together. They do this a couple of times. (Go around and help if necessary).

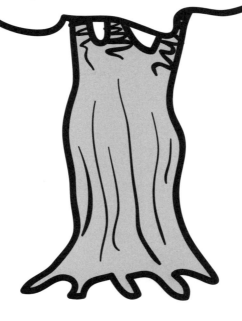

WORKSHOP No. 9

LISTENING AND ABSENCE OF LISTENING

THE WORKSHOP SCHEMA

1. **Introductory game** "the boat and the rock". Sharing impressions

2. WL comment

3. **The game of not listening**. Sharing impressions.

4. WL Comment

5. **Listening game**. Sharing impressions.

6. WL Comment

7. **Relaxing massage** in the two circles

THE GOAL of the workshop:
- To notice the different experiences of not being listened to, and being listened to;
- to become aware of the importance of attentive listening for mutual understanding.

LISTENING AND ABSENCE OF LISTENING

1. **Introductory game** "the boat and the rock".
   WL prepares in advance as many small pieces of papers as there are children. On 3 papers "The boat" is written, on the rest of them "The rock". Each child pulls out one paper, blindly. Than WL invites one of the children who picked "boat" and blindfolds him/her. All children who play "the rock" are invited to position themselves around the space. They should sit or stand in the same place till the end of a journey. The blindfolded child has the task to get from one side of the room ("the sea") to the other, passing safely among the rocks without touching them. When the boat comes close to a rock, the "rock"- child should make a sound similar to waves hitting rocks: "SH SH SH....", warning the boat to move another way. When the boat reaches the other shore, it becomes a rock, and another "boat"- child is starting its journey. After that the third boat . The rocks could change positions in the sea for each new boat.
   Sharing circle: WL is asking boats how they felt during the journey, was the sound of the waves helping them to find the way. How was it for the children representing rocks, what are their impressions.
   Question for all of them: Is there anyone wanting to comment what they learned from this game?

2. **WL COMMENT**: about the importance of sharpening our hearing and listening abilities.
   Then WL invites the children to play a game where there will be no listening, in order to experience how this feels like.

3. **The game of not listening**. Children are paired up in couples, sitting and facing each other. They agree on who is number 1 and 2 in their couple. When WL gives a sign, child No.1 starts to talk about what he/she was do-

ing during the weekend, or about a TV program he/she likes to watch, or about something she/he likes to do. While child No.2 has the task to show by mimic, gestures, position of the body that he/she is not listening at all. After 1-2 minutes, WL is asking them to switch roles. No.2 talks, No.1 does not listen.

Sharing circle: WL asks the children how it was for them to talk without being listened to. Was it difficult to talk? Was it difficult not to listen?

4. **WL COMMENT:** Now we will play a game of listening, to experience what that feels like.
   WL tells them that this time the task of the listener will be to repeat everything back, and therefore they need to listen very carefully and remember what was said.

5. **Listening game**.
   When WL gives a sign, the child No.1 starts to talk the same as before - about what he/she was doing during the weekend, or about the TV program he/she likes to watch, or about something she/he likes to do, and child No.2 is listening carefully. After 1 minute WL is saying STOP, and than child No.2 repeats back what child No.1 said.
   After they are done, WL asks them to switch roles. No.2 talks, No.1 listens.
   Sharing circle: WL asks the children how it was for them to talk while being listened to. Was it easier to talk? Was it difficult to listen? Did they succeed to repeat everything that was said?

6. **WL COMMENT**: How important it is for all of us to be listened to when we are talking, that it contributes to pleasant feelings and creates a connection between people. How important listening is for relationships in the classroom and for the process of remembering.

7. **Relaxing massage**: children are forming two circles. In each circle a child is massaging the neck and back of the child in front of him/her, and is being massaged by the child behind him/her.

APPENDIX 1
for workshop No. 10

Make a photocopy of this page and cut it along the dashed lines to make the 3 cards (A, B and C) needed for workshop no. 10.

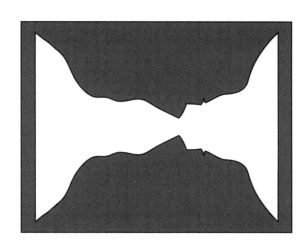

A

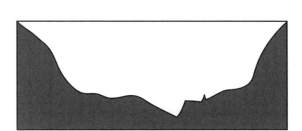

B

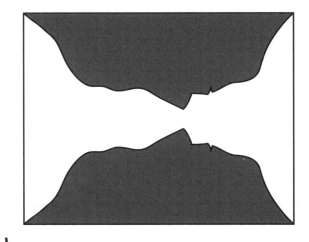

C

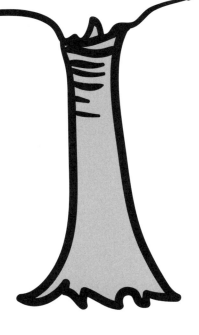

WORKSHOP No. 10

COMMUNICATION AND MISUNDERSTANDINGS (1)

THE WORKSHOP SCHEMA

1. **Circle of names** in an unusual way

2. **Abla – babla**

3. **Differences in points of view as a source of misunderstandings. Sharing around the circle**

4. **WL comment**

5. **Pantomime chain**

6. **Sharing around the circle: Why there were misunderstandings?**

THE GOAL of the workshop:
- to discover reasons of misunderstandings in communication;
- to stimulate taking the perspective of the others;
- to stimulate non-verbal communication.

COMMUNICATION AND MISUNDERSTANDINGS (1)

1. **Circle of names:** *Tell your name in an unusual way, in a way you have never done it before* (inspire them to find their own way to do this, give an example: N a a a a d a...)

2. **Abla - babla:** Pairs talk to each other in an inarticulate language, with their jaws and face muscles relaxed (cheer up exercise).

3. **Differences in points of view as a source of misunderstandings**.
   Divide them in two groups and separate them in two different corners of the room. Make the distance so that one group cannot see what the other is looking at. Show a drawing of a vase (card **A**, see appendix 1, page 37) to the first group: let it circle around until everyone has seen it. Then a drawing of profile (card **B**) is shown to the other group in the same way.
   Then put both drawings away and invite all children to sit in the circle. Go around the circle, and for a few seconds let each child see the double-drawing of the vase and the profiles (card **C**).
   Sharing around the circle: What did they see on the last drawing (everyone describes it). Then put the double drawing in the middle of the circle so everyone can see it.
   Sharing about differences in views. Why did such differences occur?

4. **WL COMMENT:**
   " Sometimes it is difficult for us to understand each other because we do not look at things from the same point of view".
   WL emphasizes the importance of knowing the other's perspective for mutual understanding.

5. **Pantomime chain:** "A" child thinks of an activity and mimes it, (e.g., spreading butter on a piece of bread). A second child tries to guess what is meant and creates his own pantomime. (e.g.: holding a cup). Now the third one guesses, and continues (pours milk into the cup) etc. No words, just pantomime. Nobody is to correct wrong guesses. When they all took their turns, there will be a discussion on what was mimed.

6. **Sharing around the circle**: What did they intended to pantomime and what came out at the end... Why there were misunderstandings?

APPENDIX 2a
for workshop No. 11

Make a photocopy of this page and cut it along the dashed lines to make the 3 cards needed for workshop no. 11 (directed drawing).

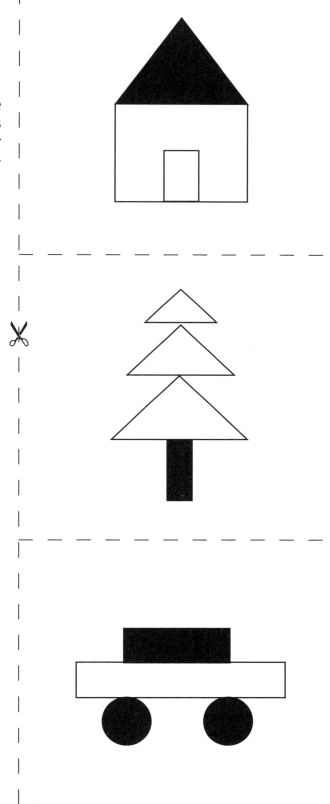

WORKSHOP No. 11

COMMUNICATION AND MISUNDERSTANDINGS (2)

THE WORKSHOP SCHEMA

1. **Circle of names:** *Tell your name in this way: Mira – Mi-pi-ra-pa...*

2. **Directed drawing in couples. Sharing** about the reasons of differences between original and copy

3. **YES-NO game: Sharing around the circle** about the strategies of persuasion

4. **WL comment**

5. **Misunderstandings with parents.** *What does your mother/father do when you say "I don't want!"?* **Sharing around the circle.**

6. **What can be done to make children and parents get along better? Sharing around the circle.**

7. **Chain of movements**

THE GOAL of the workshop:
- to discover the reasons of misunderstandings in communication;
- to stimulate taking a perspective of others;
- to stimulate nonverbal communication.

WORKSHOP No. 11

COMMUNICATION AND MISUNDERSTANDINGS (2)

1. **Circle of names:** *Tell your name in this way: Mira - Mi-pi-ra-pa...*

2. **Directed drawing:** Pairs sit back to back and close enough to be able to hear each other. "A" gets a simple drawing (see appendix 2a, page 41 and appendix 2b, page 45) and has to make "B" draw the same drawing without mentioning the names of the objects. E.g., it is a truck composed of two circles and a square, the "A" child must not spell out that it is a truck. Or, if it is a face (a circle with two smaller circles and two lines), 'a face' must not be mentioned. After they compared a model and a directed drawing, they switch roles and get a new model. **Sharing about the differences** between original and copy. Why did those differences occur? Is it difficult to make a correct drawing? Why?
   NOTE: The aim is to let children see different ways of viewing and the difficulty of communicating something to somebody who does not see what you see. The aim is not to make a perfect copy of an original.

3. **YES-NO game**. They form two rows facing each other. The first row has the task to keep saying "yes" and to get their opposite to say "yes" too. The second row has to keep saying "no" and to get their opposite to say "no" too. They all talk at the same time and they are free to use different nonverbal tricks and persuasive strategies. **Sharing:** Did they succeed in getting their partners to say what they wanted them to?

4. **WL COMMENT**: Sometimes it is difficult for us to get along with each other, because we do not want to do the things the other tries to persuade us to do (as in this game). We do not like to be forced.

5. **Misunderstandings with parents:** *what does your mother do when you say "I don't want to!"? And what does your father do when you say the same thing?* Sharing around the circle.

6. **What can be done to make children and parents get along better?**
(Let them give suggestions, show them that "I don't want to/that" can be expressed in a different way: expressing your needs preventing you to say "Yes". For example: *"I would like to decide by myself..."* **Sharing around the circle.**

7. **Chain of movements:** The leader starts with a movement and the person standing next to him "transfers" the movement to the next etc... The rule is "you look at and receive the message (movement) only from the person standing next to you, no matter what the others did". The leader introduces new movement before the previous one was performed by all children in a circle...
Movements to be sent around the circle are:
a)   snap your fingers
b)   clap your thighs
c)   clap your thighs and stomp with your feet
d)   stomp with your feet
e)   freeze

APPENDIX 2b
for workshop No. 11

Make a photocopy of this page and cut it along the dashed lines to make the 3 cards needed for workshop no. 11 (directed drawing).

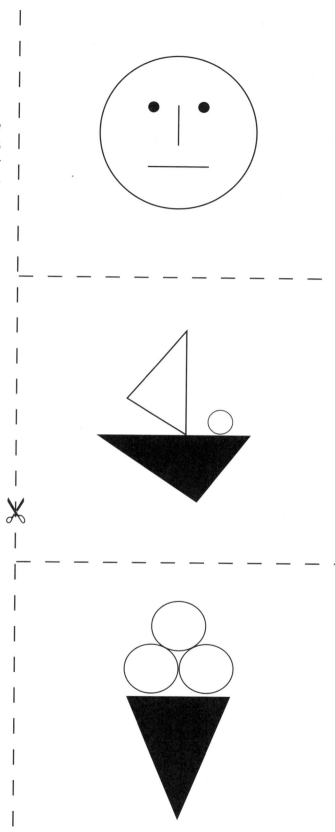

WORKSHOP No. 12

COOPERATION (1)

THE WORKSHOP SCHEMA

1. **Play with a little ball**

2. **Group drawing in silence**, without agreement

3. **Presenting the drawings**. Sharing about the experience

4. **The closing game**: Shower of pleasant messages

THE GOAL of the workshop:
- to stimulate cooperation;
- to stimulate nonverbal communication;
- To stimulate imagination.

COOPERATION (1)

1. **Play with a little ball** (or a crumbled piece of paper). They sit in a circle and throw the ball to each other, but before throwing they say the name of the person they are going to throw the ball to. Or instead of the name, they can say the color of the hair or of the eyes of the person they aim for.

2. **Group drawing in silence**. Divide children in groups of four. Their task is to create a group-project, but they are not allowed to agree on the subject in advance, or to talk while drawing. After a sign is given they all start drawing at the same time. Each has his/her own piece of paper (A4) and draws what he/she wants, without looking what the others in the group are doing. When they are finished, they agree on how to put the four drawings together. Then invite them to invent a story that will connect those four pictures, and to give a title to the whole story.

3. **Presenting the drawings.** The representative of each group presents all drawings and tells the connecting story. (Note what themes occur on the drawings.)
   Sharing in the group: Was it difficult to come to an agreement on how to put the drawings together and to think up the story?

4. **Closing game:** Shower of pleasant messages. Let the children stand in two rows facing each other. Starting from one end, a child walks between the rows. The others tell him sweet messages, smile at him or caress him. When the first child is through, he stands in the row and the next one starts, etc.

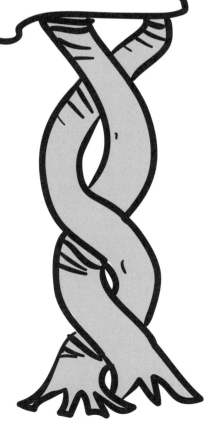

WORKSHOP No. 13

COOPERATION (2)

THE WORKSHOP SCHEMA

1. **Circle of names:** *"My name is..., and I like..."* The next child repeats

2. **Blind drawing**, presentations, sharing around the circle

3. **Carrying balloons**. Sharing around the circle about the experience

4. **Live mirror**

THE GOAL of the workshop:
- cooperation;
- nonverbal communication;
- Imagination.

COOPERATION (2)

1. **Circle of names:** *"My name is Mira, and I like..."* The next child repeats: *"Mira likes... and my name is Dejan and I like..."* and so on. Every child repeats the name and the statement of the previous one.

2. **Blind drawing:** form groups of 7-8. Give each group a piece of paper (20 cm x 150 cm). One child in each group starts drawing. The others are not allowed to see what is drawn. That child draws a part of a theme or a being, and then folds the paper so that his drawing can not be seen. Only a little bit sticks out, so the next child knows were to continue to draw, starting at the visible ends of the lines. And the game continues this way, until the group reaches the end of the taped paper. At the end, they unfold the paper, look at the outcome, and give a title to the joint-drawing. **Presentation:** Group representatives show drawings and name titles. **Sharing around the circle:** How did they feel during this game?

3. **Carrying balloons:** form pairs. Put 2-3 blown-up balloons on ribbons (paper or cloth, 8-10 cm wide). The pairs have to carry the balloons on the ribbons across the room without letting the balloons fall down (each partner holds one end of the ribbon). **Sharing in the group:** What was difficult, what did they do in order to keep the balloons from falling down?

4. **Live mirror:** the whole group plays this game at the same time. Pairs stand facing each other. The fist partner thinks of an activity (e.g., combing hair) and starts slowly to pantomime the movement. The second one imitates him as if he was his reflection in the mirror. The first one adds new movements, while the other one keeps on imitating him like a mirror, so that at the end you can't say who acts and who mirrors. Switch the roles.

WORKSHOP No. 14

DREAMS

THE WORKSHOP SCHEMA

1. **Pantomime game**: Eating.

2. **What do you dream about?** Sharing around the circle.

3. **Draw your most terrible dream**.

4. **Draw your most beautiful dream**. Sharing around the circle.

5. **Performing dreams in small groups**. Audience comments.

6. **Closing game**: sitting on thighs in circle

THE GOAL of the workshop:
- To let them express inner contents;
- To stimulate imagination;
- To stimulate cooperation.

WORKSHOP No. 14

DREAMS

1. **Pantomime game: Eating**. Do a pantomime pretending you are eating something. First think of what you are going to "eat". Then show how you do that. The others try to guess what you are eating. Then move to the next child in the circle, even if the guesses were wrong.

2. **What do you dream about?** When we sleep we sometimes dream of something pleasant, sometimes of something unpleasant or terrifying. **Sharing around the circle:** What did you dream in the last days: pleasant or unpleasant?

3. **Draw your most terrible dream**. After they finish it:

4. **Draw your most beautiful dream.**
   Sharing around the circle: Each child shows his drawings and explains them.

5. **Performing dreams:** *Let us now make a performance from your dreams. We will form 4 groups. Each group will decide together which events from their dreams they are going to play and how.* (Let each group choose freely what they want to perform from their beautiful, and their terrible dreams. Help them not to argue about casting. Encourage them to add to the play something new, which was not on the drawings. Let them rehears. After each group's performance, the audience comments: what they liked, what they did not like, how they liked the ending. Encourage them to find positive, optimistic solutions if they did not already do that.)

6. **Closing:** They all stand in a tight circle, *facing each other's backs, their left feet point towards the next child. They are so close to each other that one child's left foot touches the left foot of the one in front of him as well as the one standing behind. Then everybody sits down at the same time so that they come to sit on the thighs of the one standing behind. If the exercise is done right, they can even try to slowly move that way in union.

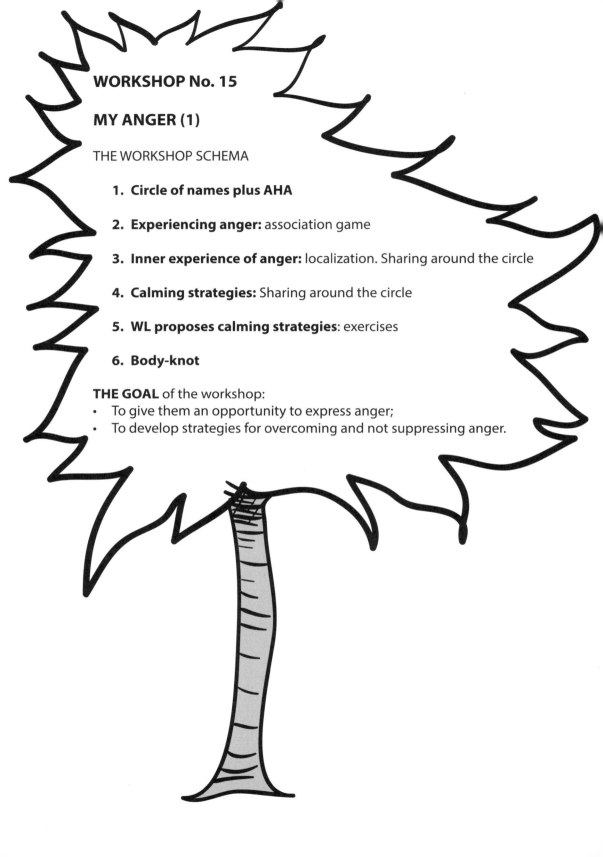

WORKSHOP No. 15

MY ANGER (1)

THE WORKSHOP SCHEMA

1. **Circle of names plus AHA**

2. **Experiencing anger:** association game

3. **Inner experience of anger:** localization. Sharing around the circle

4. **Calming strategies:** Sharing around the circle

5. **WL proposes calming strategies**: exercises

6. **Body-knot**

THE GOAL of the workshop:
- To give them an opportunity to express anger;
- To develop strategies for overcoming and not suppressing anger.

MY ANGER (1)

1. **Circle of names:** *Say your name as loud as you can, shout it... Then shout your name and add a loud and sharp "A-HA!" (For example Mara-A-Ha!).*

2. **Experiencing anger:** association game around the circle - quickly continue the sentences: *I am angry as a ... When I am angry..., I feel like ... (exploding).*

3. **Inner experience of anger:** localization. *We all are sometimes mad and angry. Close your eyes and try to remember how you felt when you were angry or mad: where in your body does the anger start to grow, how does it spread, what places does it reach?*
Sharing around the circle: *Where in your body do you feel anger, where does it start, how does it spread, how far does it reach?*

4. **Calming strategies:** Sharing around the circle - *When you are mad, how do you regain your calm? What do you do, what do you think about? How do you calm yourself most easily?*

5. **WL propose calming strategies :** *Let's see what we can do when we are mad to express ourselves fully, but not to hurt ourselves nor others:*
    a) *madly squeeze a towel;*
    b) *hit the bed with a towel or with hands and shout;*
    c) *doodle*: give them paper for expressing their anger with mad doodling (they can draw a thing/person which/who makes them mad and then scrub over it, or they can crumple the paper up and then throw it away as far as they can);
    d) *Make a lion's roar -- sit down on your knees, with feet tucked under. Put your hands on your knees. Then open your mouth, relax the face muscles, stick out your tongue as far as possible and let the air flow out from your lungs in silence. Then repeat that but let a scream come out from the bottom of your lungs, just like a lion;*
    e) *Relaxation exercise - sit down, breathe slowly, imagine that from the top of your head a wave of relaxation flows and it envelops you reaching your toes.*

6. **Body-knot:** Standing in a circle, they hold each others hands. Then they form a human knot, hands held tightly, twisting around each other, crawling under each other's arms until they cannot move anymore. Then they try to untangle, with hand still holding.

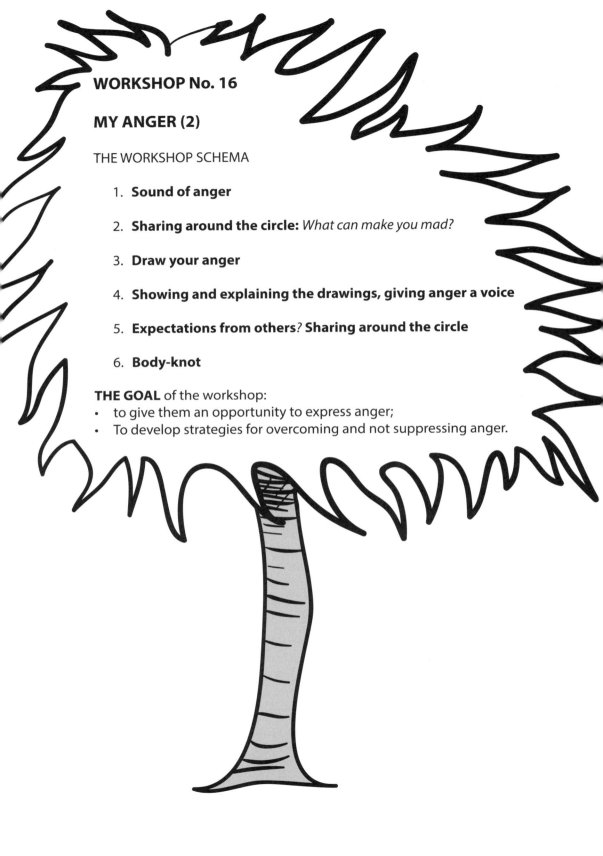

WORKSHOP No. 16

MY ANGER (2)

THE WORKSHOP SCHEMA

1. **Sound of anger**

2. **Sharing around the circle:** *What can make you mad?*

3. **Draw your anger**

4. **Showing and explaining the drawings, giving anger a voice**

5. **Expectations from others***?* **Sharing around the circle**

6. **Body-knot**

THE GOAL of the workshop:
- to give them an opportunity to express anger;
- To develop strategies for overcoming and not suppressing anger.

WORKSHOP No. 16

MY ANGER (2)

1. **Sound of anger:** *Find the sound or syllable that is expressing your anger in the best way. It could be a hissing sound "ssss" or growling "grrrr". Lets make that sound together, each of us in their own way!*

2. **Sharing around the circle:** *What can make you mad?*

3. **Draw your anger:** *Give your anger a shape and color(s)*
   Sharing around the circle: Showing and explaining of the drawings. After a child presents his drawing, ask: *Now be that drawing and give your anger a voice. What does your anger sound like? What does your anger say about itself?*

4. **Expectations from the others:** *What would you like others to do when you are mad?* **Sharing around the circle.** *And what do they usually do?* Sharing around the circle. How can you change that? Sharing around the circle.

5. **Body-knot:** Standing in a circle, they hold each others hands. Then they form a human knot, hands held tightly, twisting around each other, crawling under each other's arms until they cannot move anymore. Then they try to untangle, with hand still holding.

55

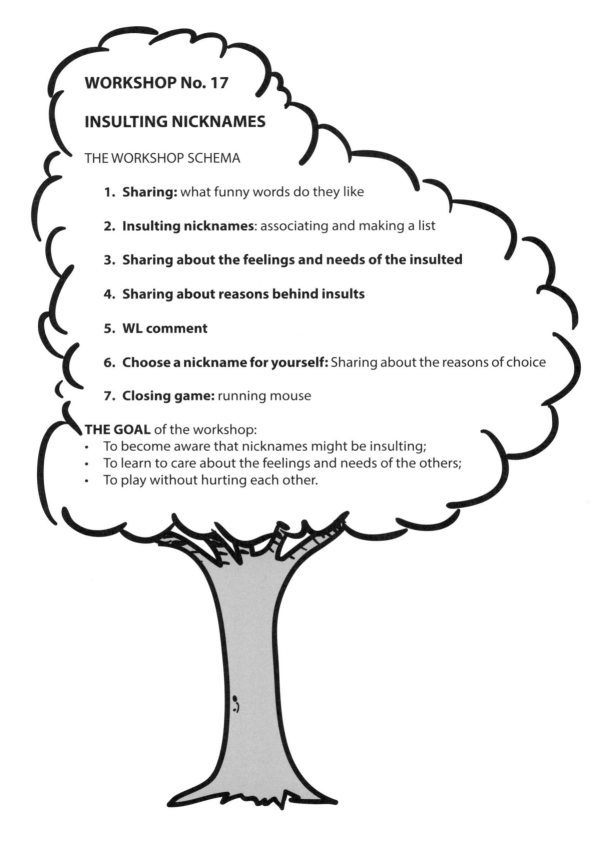

WORKSHOP No. 17

INSULTING NICKNAMES

THE WORKSHOP SCHEMA

1. **Sharing:** what funny words do they like

2. **Insulting nicknames**: associating and making a list

3. **Sharing about the feelings and needs of the insulted**

4. **Sharing about reasons behind insults**

5. **WL comment**

6. **Choose a nickname for yourself:** Sharing about the reasons of choice

7. **Closing game:** running mouse

THE GOAL of the workshop:
- To become aware that nicknames might be insulting;
- To learn to care about the feelings and needs of the others;
- To play without hurting each other.

INSULTING NICKNAMES

1. What funny words do they like
   WL is reading the verse of D. Radovic's poem: *Children like some funny words*.
   WL can choose any English short text speaking about playing with funny words and names.
   Sharing in the group: *What funny words do you like?* WL is inviting children to associate freely...

2. **Insulting nicknames**
   WL: There *are some words you may find funny, but they are insulting for the others. Nicknames, for example. What are the nicknames you do not like, or you find them insulting in regards your friends?*
   Children say the nicknames and WL is writing them on the board. If the children know how to write, they can write insulting nicknames on small pieces of paper.

3. **Sharing feelings and needs of the insulted**
   WL is reads what is written on the papers, or on the board, one nickname after the other, and asks children to guess how the child receiving this nickname (e.g., "Fat", "blind") is feeling? Why is he/she is feeling like that, what does she/he need?
   WL is inviting children to imagine how they would feel and why, if they would experience this. What need would not be met (because they have a need to be appreciated by peers, to be accepted etc.). **Sharing in the group.**

4. **Sharing about reasons behind insults**
   Why are children giving nicknames to others?
   How could you have fun without hurting each other?

5. **WL COMMENT**: When you invent some nickname for the other it is important to check how the other is feeling about it. And if you see that it is not pleasant for the other, do not use that nickname.

6. **Choose a nickname you like**:
   WL is asking children to share what nickname they would like to have, and why.
   Sharing around the circle: about the choice, and the reasons for the choice.

7. **Closing game: running mouse**
   Children are in the circle. WL is asking them to imagine that one little mouse is running around the circle, from the left to the right. So when the mouse reaches the place where they are, they need to raise the left foot first, than right foot to let the mouse pass. The game goes in several turns, speeding up with every turn...

WORKSHOP No. 18

TELLTALE

THE WORKSHOP SCHEMA

1. **Telltale in the classroom. Role play** in small groups
   Sharing after each role play: how they were feeling, what needs were not met (the children's and the teacher's)

2. **WL Comment**

3. **Sharing in the big group**: what kind of misunderstandings could the children resolve among themselves, without reporting to the teacher? How?

4. **Role play in the small groups**: transforming telltale in 3 steps
   Sharing in the big group: was that a satisfactory and realistic solution? How did they come to that solution?

5. Making a list of peer behaviors that are bothering them.
   Sharing in the big group: teacher writing the list on the board

6. The sign of feeling: drawings. Sharing about the drawings

THE GOAL of the workshop:
- To recognize their own and other's feelings and needs;
- To take responsibility to resolve misunderstandings and conflicts among peers.

WORKSHOP No. 18

TELLTALE

1. **Telltale in the classroom**
   Role play in the small groups: children are divided in small groups, 5 children in each group. Four of them are playing children, one is playing a teacher. Each group has the task to prepare a presentation for the big group about one case of telltale. Some of them are playing the child/children reporting against others to the teacher. The child playing the role of the teacher is trying to make peace among them, in a way he/she chooses.
   Sharing after each role play: WL is asking every participant in the role plays how they were feeling, what needs of theirs were not met.

2. **WL COMMENT**: telltale is not helping to change what is bothering you, it is contributing that we all feel dissatisfied. The teacher is dissatisfied because he/she loves to see harmony and friendship among students, and to be sure that they can resolve misunderstandings on their own, without telling to the teacher.

3. **Sharing in the big group**: what kind of their misunderstandings could the children resolve without reporting to the teacher? How?

4. **Transforming telltale.**
   Role play in the small groups: Children are again in the same groups as in the first role play. This time the task is:
   a. *to try to express directly to the child whose behavior is bothering you how you are feeling and what need of yours is not met when he/she is doing what is bothering you.*
   b. *to try to guess why that child is doing it, what he/she is feeling and needing. Check by asking "Are you feeling...because you want...?*
   c. *to try to find a way of meeting needs so that everybody could be satisfied*
   Sharing in the big group: was that a satisfactory and realistic solution? How did they come to that solution?

5. **Making a list of peer behaviors that are bothering them**.
   WL says: *Let us make a list of behaviors of your peers that are bothering you. Remember something, you do not like in the behavior of your classmates*
   Sharing in the big group: teacher writes the list on the board.

6. **The sign of feeling**: drawings
   WL: *make some kind of sign that will remind you to directly express to the one whose behavior is bothering you how you are feeling. What could you draw, that would serve that purpose? It is important that it is your own unique sign*...Children are drawing.

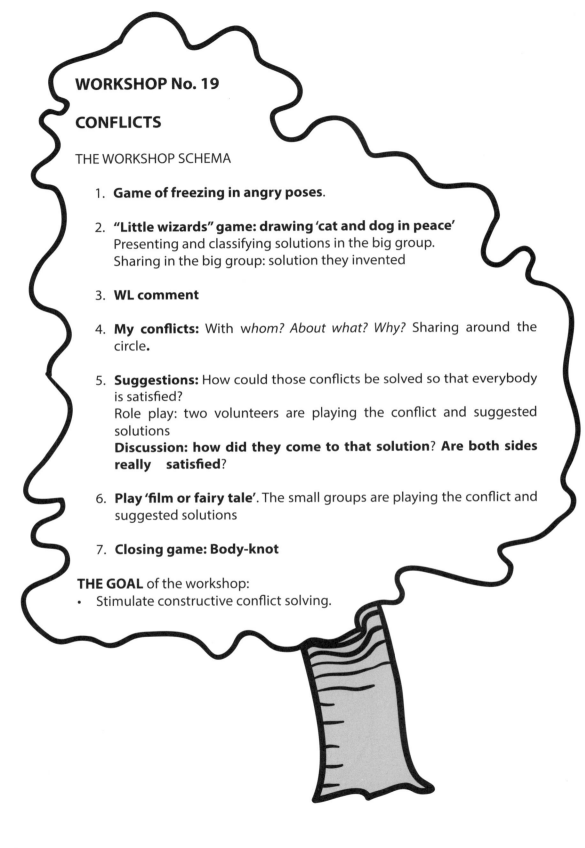

WORKSHOP No. 19

CONFLICTS

THE WORKSHOP SCHEMA

1. **Game of freezing in angry poses**.

2. **"Little wizards" game: drawing 'cat and dog in peace'**
   Presenting and classifying solutions in the big group.
   Sharing in the big group: solution they invented

3. **WL comment**

4. **My conflicts:** With *whom? About what? Why?* Sharing around the circle.

5. **Suggestions:** How could those conflicts be solved so that everybody is satisfied?
   Role play: two volunteers are playing the conflict and suggested solutions
   Discussion: how did they come to that solution? **Are both sides really satisfied**?

6. **Play 'film or fairy tale'**. The small groups are playing the conflict and suggested solutions

7. **Closing game: Body-knot**

THE GOAL of the workshop:
· Stimulate constructive conflict solving.

WORKSHOP No. 19

CONFLICTS

1. **Game of freezing in angry pose**.
   Children move around the room bumping into each other. When a sign is given, they "freeze" in angry or mad positions. WL goes from child to child, 'unfreezes' one by one and asks each child: *"Who are you right now? Why are you feeling that way?"*

2. **"Little wizards" game: drawings.**
   Tell the children to imagine that they have magic powers and that they can do whatever they want. How would they solve the cat-dog problem? Ask them to draw their solutions to the problem. How would they bring dogs and cats to live in peace? What would they do to them, how would they change them, or what would they give them in order to make them live in peace? (Encourage them to search for their own solutions, to use their imagination.)
   Then categorize those drawings and compare them. Here are some variations of solutions given by children of that age: tying them up, closing them in the two cages, putting up walls; to create a mixed animal with characteristics of both animals; to give to each of them what they like; to introduce a third person, a mediator; to raise them together from birth; a magic wand that would make them love each other...).
   Sharing around the circle: Which solution did they come up with?

3. **WL COMMENT:** WL points out that in every conflict it is necessary that both sides change a little and consider the other's needs.

4. **My conflicts:** *Whom do you argue with most? About what? Why?*
   Sharing around the circle. WL is suggesting to the children to focus on the needs of the conflicting parties.

5. **Suggestions: How could those conflicts be solved so that everybody is satisfied?** *Our conflicts usually end up in the way that one wins and the other looses, or both loose or both loose a little and win a little. We will now look for a creative solution that would satisfy all.*

(They choose one typical conflict and the leader asks for two volunteers to play roles. First, they act out the conflict as it really happened. Then the group suggests a constructive solution to the problem.) *How could that conflict be solved in a new way that would satisfy both sides?* Volunteers should play out each suggested solution.

Discussion: how did they come to that solution? Are both sides really satisfied?

6. **Play film or fairy tale.** If there are some difficulties: encourage them to imagine how the conflict would be solved in a comedy or in a fairy tale. Children are working in small groups, choosing one conflict and presenting it like a scene from the movie or fairy tale where anything is possible.

7. **Closing game: Body-knot**. 7-8 children form a circle, close their eyes, put their arms in front of them and reach for the hands of the others. When every hand holds another hand, they open their eyes and try to untangle. The rule of the game demands that everything be done in silence, without speaking.

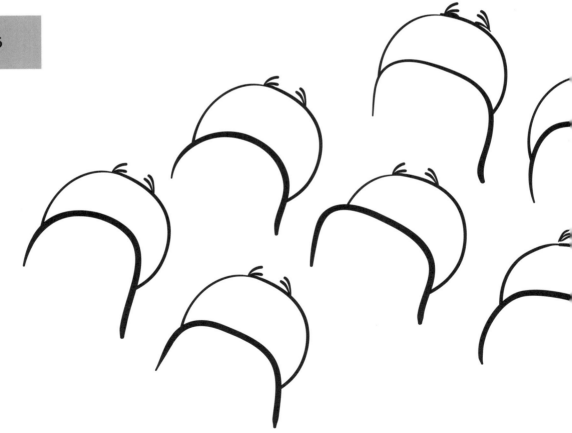

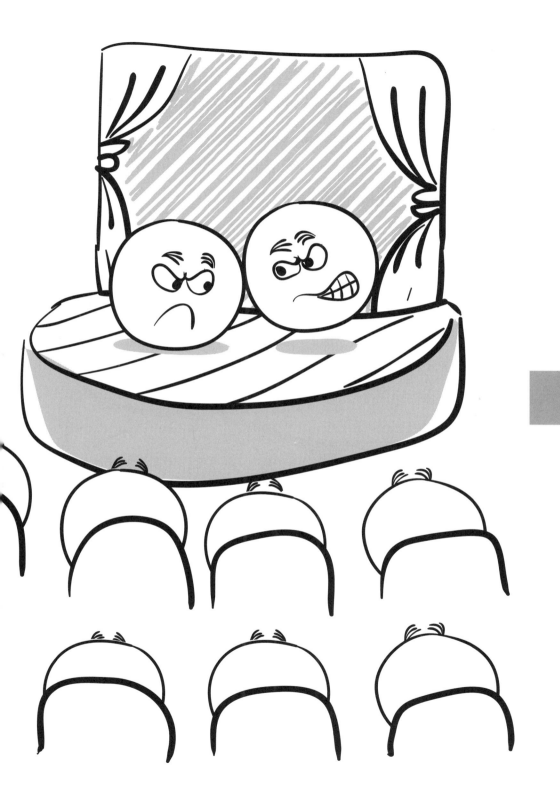

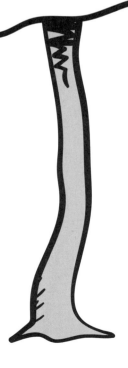

WORKSHOP No. 20

FEARS (1)

THE WORKSHOP SCHEMA

1. **Suspense walk,** Sharing around the circle about that experience

2. **Experiencing fear: association game**

3. **Inner experience of fear:** localization. **Sharing around the circle**

4. **WL comment**

5. **Strategies against fear. Sharing around the circle.**

THE GOAL of the workshop:
- To give children an opportunity to express and share their fears;
- To develop strategies for overcoming and not suppressing fear;
- To stimulate imagination;
- To stimulate cooperation and sharing.

FEARS (1)

1. **Suspense walk**: all children choose a spot in the room and stand there, keeping some 40-60 cm of distance between them. After a sign is given, they close their eyes and start walking around, wherever they want. They do that **in silence and keep their arms close to the body**. At the "STOP!" sign they freeze and, **without touching and eyes still closed, try to guess** how many persons are around them and what the approximate distance to them is. Help them by saying: *Try to guess if there is anybody behind you, on your left, on your right, in front of you. But don't open your eyes!* After 20 seconds, they can open their eyes and verify the correctness of their guesses. Repeated the game twice.

   NOTE: Pay attention to the way they move, how safely they seem to move, do they crowd together or move freely, do they touch each other or hold their arms in front of them, do they giggle or whisper? In short, note if there are any signs of anxiety.

   Sharing around the circle: How did they feel during this walk? Did they feel any fear and if they did, fear of what? Were their guesses correct?

2. **Experiencing fear: association game** around the circle. Quickly complete:
   - *I am scared like a...* (Rabbit etc.)
   - *I got...* (Frozen etc.) *with fear*
   - *When I am scared, I feel like...* (Screaming etc.)

3. **Inner experience of fear:** localization. They get an outline of the human body, just contours. *Draw in that body where you feel fear when you are scared. Where does it start, where does it spread to, and which color would it be, how intense, which size... Try to express that using colors.*

   Sharing around the circle: *How and where do they feel fear?* (They show and explain their drawings.)

4. **WL COMMENT:** *When we talk about fear we usually think of the fear that's bothering us. But some fears can help us, because they warn us to avoid danger* (for example, motor-car horn, sudden movement...)

5. **Strategies against fear:**
   How do you fight against fear? What do you do to get rid of it? **Sharing around the circle.**

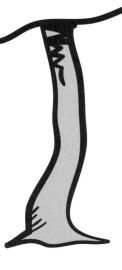

WORKSHOP No. 21

FEARS (2)

THE WORKSHOP SCHEMA

1. **Circle of names:** *Whisper fearfully.*

2. **Remember** situations, beings, things, people you are afraid of.

3. **Draw what you fear the most**. Sharing around the circle.

4. **Helper against fear**. Sharing around the circle. What is the helper, how does it work?

5. **Shield against fear: small group work. Sharing:** Group representatives show and explain shields.

6. **Closing: ZOOM-BA.**

THE GOAL of the workshop:
- To give children an opportunity to express and share their fears;
- To develop strategies for overcoming and not suppressing fear;
- To develop a positive approach to problems;
- To stimulate imagination;
- To stimulate sharing and cooperation.

FEARS (2)

1. **Circle of names:** *Whisper your name as if you were scared.*

2. **Remember:** *Close your eyes and try to think of a situation, creature, thing, event or person that scares or scared you (1 min).*

3. **Draw what you fear the most.** Sharing around the circle: *What makes you scared? What are you afraid of?*

4. **What can we do to overcome the fear that bothers us:** *We can use our imagination against fear. Close your eyes. Now imagine you had a helper who will take care of all the things that scare you unnecessarily. It can be a creature from a fairy tale, or a real person, or an imaginary person, or a thing... It is important to think of a way in which you will call for them or it when you need help.* **Sharing around the circle:** *Who or what is your helper? How does it work?*

5. **Shield against fear:** *Now, in groups of 4, we are going to make shields against fear for ourselves. The shield should contain all the things that help us to conquer fear. You could try to draw what you are afraid of a lot and add to it something, which will transform that picture and make it funny... Or you can draw your helper... You decide what your shield will look like... Give a large piece of paper to each group. They will do this as they like: each can draw in his own corner, or they can first decide what they are going to draw and do it together...* **Sharing:** Group representatives show and explain shields.

6. **Closing game: ZOOM-BA.** *You say "Zoom" and the person sitting next to you has to say "zoom" quickly, then passes the word on to the person sitting next to him, and so on, until somebody says "Ba!". Then the "Zoom" travels back around the circle, until somebody else says "Ba!" And so on.*

WORKSHOP No. 22

SADNESS

THE WORKSHOP SCHEMA

1. Draw a **sad face**.

2. **What makes you sad? Sharing around the circle.**

3. **Inner experience of sadness:** localization. Sharing around the circle.

4. **What do you usually do when you are sad?** Do you like to be alone or you ask somebody to be with you? Whom do you ask that? **Sharing around the circle.**

5. Do you cry easily? When did you cry the last time? Sharing around the circle.

6. **WL comment**

7. **Smile to yourself.** Sharing around the circle: *How do you feel now?*

8. **What do you do in order not to feel sad?** Sharing around the **circle.**

9. **How can others cheer you up***! Friends? Parents?* Sharing.

10. **Modeling game:** sculptors/sculptures.

11. **Sharing around the circle:** How did they feel playing sculptors/ sculptures? Did they feel a shift in their mood; if yes, at what point?

12. **Group sculpture** of joy.

THE GOAL of the workshop:
- To give children an opportunity to express and share sadness;
- To develop strategies for overcoming sadness;
- To stimulate friendship.

WORKSHOP No. 22

SADNESS

1. *Draw a **sad face**.* Each child is drawing.

2. **What makes you sad? Sharing around the circle.**

3. **Inner experience of sadness. Localization.** *Where in your body do you feel sadness? Which color would your sadness be?* (They get human body contours and mark on them where and how they experience sadness). **Sharing around the circle.** *Where do they feel sadness? How does it look like?*

4. **What do you usually do when you are sad?** *Do you like to be alone or you ask somebody to be with you? Whom do you ask that?*

5. **Do you cry easily?**
   WL comment: It is good to cry**.** *Crying calms, relaxes**. When did you cry lately?* **Sharing around the circle.**

6. **WL comment:** It is important to know how to smile to yourself also. *Let's try:*

7. **Close you eyes and smile. Keep that expression until I say "It is OK"** (let them smile for a minute).
   Sharing around the circle: *How do you feel now?*

8. **What do you do in order to not feel sad?**
   Sharing around the circle.

9. **How can others cheer you up***! Friends? Parents?* **Sharing.**

10. **Modeling:** *How else can we help each other to feel better?* (Form two groups. Children from one group get up and make "sculptures of sadness",

i.e. take poses they usually take when they are sad. The second group has the task to model the "sad sculptures" in order to make "happy figures" out of them. Each sculptor can make **one change** at each sculpture to make it joyful. Sculptors can move sculptures' hands, legs, neck, head, etc. After a sculptor makes a change at one sculpture, he moves to next one, and so on.) When all the sculptors are through, they evaluate their work; try to see if they are satisfied with their mutual work of art. (Sculptures stand still all that time - about 7 minutes.) Then they change roles and the game starts over. (About 7 minutes.)

Sharing around the circle: How did they feel playing sculptors, and how did they feel playing sculptures? Did they, and if yes, when did they feel a shift in their mood?

11.**Closing game:** *Let's model joy together. They all make a sculpture of joy together.* (Take a photo if possible!)

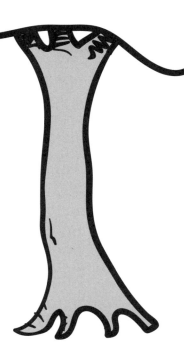

WORKSHOP No. 23

MY WISHES

THE WORKSHOP SCHEMA

1. **Show with your body how you are feeling.**

2. **What do you usually do to get what you want? How do you ask for it from the parents? Sharing around the circle.**

3. **Wish fulfilling fairy**: Imagining and drawing their wishes. Sharing around the circle: How they were feeling? What is their wish?

4. **Making wish posters.**

5. **Magic machine: imagining, drawing. Sharing around the circle.**

6. **Closing circle:** *When I am happy, I feel like...*

THE GOAL of the workshop:
· To stimulate imagination and positive feelings.

MY WISHES

1. **Show with your body how you are feeling:** A child does that and all the others simultaneously imitate, copying posture, facial expression, movement.

2. **What do you usually do to get what you want?** *How do you ask your parents for what you want?* **Sharing around the circle.**

3. **Wish fulfilling fairy:** *Close your eyes. Imagine that you have just met a* wish fulfilling *fairy. What would you wish for? Open your eyes and draw your wish.* **Sharing around the circle:** *How did they feel during this exercise? What was their wish?*

4. **Making wish posters.**
   All their wishes are being put on the wall (similar or complement wishes can be put in groups).

5. **Magic machine:** *Close your eyes again and imagine a magic machine that can fulfill your wishes. How does that wish-machine look like? What can it do? Which wishes can it fulfill? How do you turn it on? First you create it in your imagination, and then you draw it.* **Presenting and commenting drawings in a circle**

6. **Closing:** *When I am happy, I feel like... flying...or...* (First they say it, and then, in a second turn, they show with their bodies how happy they are).

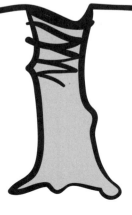

WORKSHOP No. 24

ME AND HOW OTHERS SEE ME

THE WORKSHOP SCHEMA

1. **Which sounds can your body produce?** Showing, imitating.

2. **Make your self-portrait** plus cloud of feelings.

3. **Comparing this self-portrait with the one from the second workshop**:
   Sharing around the circle: Presenting and commenting the drawings. What has changed? Why did it change? Sharing around the circle.

4. **Draw yourself the way you would like to look like when you grow up**.
   Sharing around the circle: Presenting and commenting the drawings.

5. **What do you like about yourself**? Sharing around the circle.

6. **What do your mother/father like the most about you?** Sharing around the circle.

7. **What do your friends like about you**? Sharing around the circle.

8. **Confidence exercises** – squat and stand up in pairs.

THE GOAL of the workshop:
- To make children aware of themselves, their qualities, similarities and differences.

WORKSHOP No. 24

ME AND HOW OTHERS SEE ME

1. *Which sounds can your body produce?* A child, which discovers a way that his body can make a sound, raises his hand and shows that action, and the others repeat it (snapping fingers, clapping hands...).

2. *Draw yourself* on this paper (A4 sheet): **make your self-portrait**. *Draw so it shows that it is you*. When they finish drawing, say: *And now, in a cloud* (remind them of clouds in cartoons where it says what a character thinks) *show how you feel today, what mood you are in, using colors the way you like. Choose colors that express what you feel. If your mood has changed since this morning, show that with different colors*. When they all finish this work:

3. **Comparing this self portrait with the one from the second workshop**
   Now give them their self-portraits from the 2.workshop.
   Sharing around the circle: *Show us and describe what you have drawn. What has changed in you   from the second workshop till now? Why did it change?*

4. **Draw yourself the way you would like to look like when you grow up.**
   What would you like to have changed by that time?
   Sharing around the circle: *Show and describe your drawings.*

5. **What do you like about yourself?** *Which of your traits do you like?*
   Sharing around the circle.

6. *What do you think your mother likes the most about you? And your father?*
   Sharing around the circle.

7. *What do your friends like about you?* **Sharing around the circle.**

8. **Confidence exercises** - pairs stand back-to-back holding each other by the elbows and squat and stand up several times.

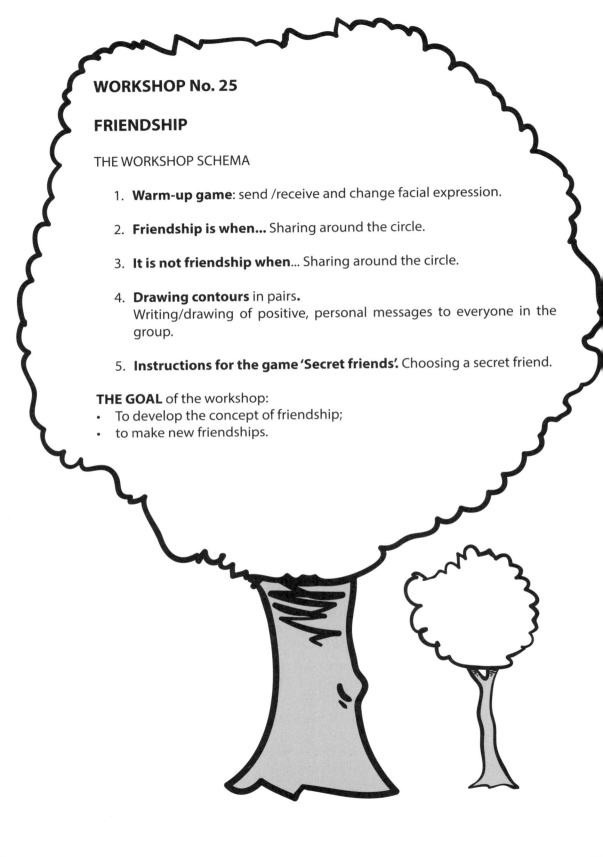

WORKSHOP No. 25

FRIENDSHIP

THE WORKSHOP SCHEMA

1. **Warm-up game**: send /receive and change facial expression.

2. **Friendship is when...** Sharing around the circle.

3. **It is not friendship when**... Sharing around the circle.

4. **Drawing contours** in pairs.
   Writing/drawing of positive, personal messages to everyone in the group.

5. **Instructions for the game 'Secret friends'.** Choosing a secret friend.

THE GOAL of the workshop:
- To develop the concept of friendship;
- to make new friendships.

FRIENDSHIP

1. **Warming up game**: send/receive and change facial expressions. WL is starting by showing the child next to him some unusual facial expression. The child repeats it and then adds something of his own, then 'sends' it to the next child in the circle, and so on.

2. **Association game:** Friendship is when... Sharing of opinions and experiences with friendship in the circle

3. **Association game**: It is not friendship when... Sharing in the circle: situations and behaviors that are illustrating a lack of, or the opposite of friendship

4. **Drawing of the contours**: children are in pairs. First one, then the other is drawing the contours of the body of each other. (One is lying on a big paper, the other one draws a contour around the body, and then they switch roles). Than each child is writing his name on his contour.
   Activity in the group: every child is writing, or drawing some friendly, personal message inside the contours of all other children

5. **Instructions for the game 'Secret friends'**. WL is informing the children that they will be invited to pick one piece of paper from the box. On each paper is the name of one child from their class. This name is a secret to the others. Only the child who picked it knows it, and he is supposed to be the secret friend to the child, whose name he picked till the next workshop: To send him/her some little signs of attention (drawings, friendly messages, sweets, or whatever they like), to help him, to make him joyful. But conspiracy is very crucial for the game: they need to take care not to be recognized, to stay secret. So they need to send the gifts secretly, asking someone else to give it to the friend he picked, or leave it on his/her chair secretly... with a message "from your secret friend".

Choosing a secret friend:

WL has written the names of all children in the class on small pieces of paper and put them in a box. If there are an uneven number of children in a group, WL puts his own name in the box. One child after the other takes a paper, and secretly reads the name of the friend he chose for the time till the next workshop. After they read the names in secret, they hide the paper so that it stays a secret. If a child should pick out his own name, he puts it back into the box and takes another paper.

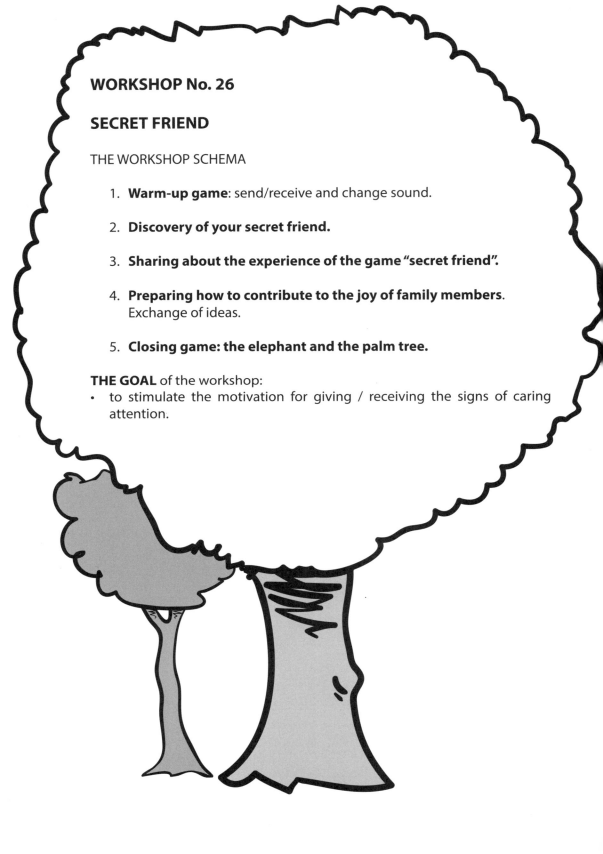

WORKSHOP No. 26

SECRET FRIEND

THE WORKSHOP SCHEMA

1. **Warm-up game**: send/receive and change sound.

2. **Discovery of your secret friend.**

3. **Sharing about the experience of the game "secret friend".**

4. **Preparing how to contribute to the joy of family members**.
   Exchange of ideas.

5. **Closing game: the elephant and the palm tree.**

THE GOAL of the workshop:
- to stimulate the motivation for giving / receiving the signs of caring attention.

SECRET FRIEND

1. **Warming up game**: send/receive and change sound. WL produces some unusual sound and sends it to the child next to him; the child is repeating the sound and then adding some sound of his own and sends it to the child next to him in the circle, and so on.

2. **Discovering who your secret friend was**. All participants are sitting in a circle. One child enters the center of the circle and stands there with closed eyes. Then his secret friend joins him. The child in the center tries to guess who it is by touching the face of his secret friend, still with the eyes closed. After he discovered who the secret friend is, the first child stands back in the circle, and the secret friend closes his eyes, and gets to guess who his friend was; and so on.

3. **Sharing about the experience** of the game "secret friend": children are sharing how it was for them to think up what would make their chosen friends happy, what they did, how they felt receiving the messages/gifts from their secret friends.

4. **Preparing how to contribute to the joy of family members**. Exchange of ideas.
   Children are associating and sharing ideas about how they can contribute to the joy of their parents, siblings, relatives. They are choosing whom they want to surprise and how, and share it with the group.

5. **Closing game: the elephant and the palm tree.**
   All children are standing in a circle. One child is standing in the middle of the circle, pointing a finger toward one child after the other, saying "elephant" or "palm tree". The child designated as "elephant" bends down, putting the arms together imitating the trunk of the elephant. The children standing on his left and right are raising the left/right hand, imitating the ears of the elephant.
   The child, designated as "palm tree" raises both arms, and the children standing on his left and right are bending their arms, imitating the branches of the palm tree.

85

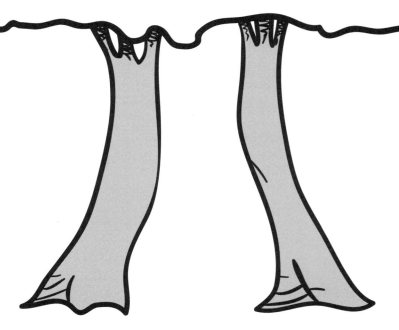

WORKSHOP No. 27

LOVE

THE WORKSHOP SCHEMA

1. **Circle of names:** Say your name tenderly.

2. **Associations:** *Love is when... Love is not when...*

3. **Expressing love only with eyes, mouth, face, hands, body: Showing around the circle.**

4. **Localizing the feeling of love.**
   Sharing around the circle: Where in your body do you feel love? How does it look like?

5. **Signs of love:** *How would you like others to show you their love.*

6. **Closing game:** *Say something pleasant to a person sitting next to you.*

THE GOAL of the workshop:
• To make children differentiate and express the experience of love.

LOVE

1. **Circle of names:** *Say your name tenderly.*

2. **Associations:** *Love is when... Love is not when...*

3. **Expressing love - showing around the circle**: *How would you express your love using:*
   - only eyes
   - only mouth
   - whole face
   - hands
   - whole body

4. ***Where in your body do you feel love?*** *Which color would your love be?* They get human body contours and mark on it where and how they experience love. **Sharing around the circle:** *Where do you feel love? How does it look like?*

5. **Signs of love:** *How would you like others to show you their love? Mother, father, boys, girls...?*

6. **Closing game:** *Say something pleasant to a person sitting next to you.*

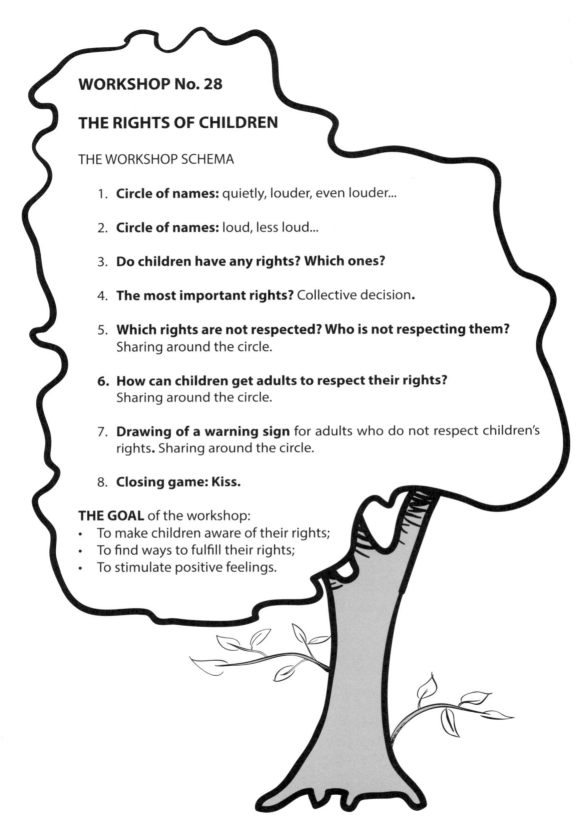

WORKSHOP No. 28

THE RIGHTS OF CHILDREN

THE WORKSHOP SCHEMA

1. **Circle of names:** quietly, louder, even louder...

2. **Circle of names:** loud, less loud...

3. **Do children have any rights? Which ones?**

4. **The most important rights?** Collective decision.

5. **Which rights are not respected? Who is not respecting them?**
Sharing around the circle.

6. **How can children get adults to respect their rights?**
Sharing around the circle.

7. **Drawing of a warning sign** for adults who do not respect children's
rights. Sharing around the circle.

8. **Closing game: Kiss.**

THE GOAL of the workshop:
- To make children aware of their rights;
- To find ways to fulfill their rights;
- To stimulate positive feelings.

THE RIGHTS OF CHILDREN

1. **Circle of names:** The first child says his/hers name quietly, the second one a little bit louder, the third one still louder, and so on.

2. **Circle of names:** The first child shouts his/her name, the second one says it a little bit less loud, and so on.

3. *Do children have any rights? Which ones?* **Sharing around the circle.**

4. **The most important rights**: they decide in the group which rights of children are the most important ones. WL help them if needed: *A child has a right to play, to eat what he likes, to be with those he loves, to have his own opinion, to ask what he wants to know, to have friends, to learn, to get help when he needs it...*

5. *Which are your rights that others do not respect? Who does not respect those rights?* **Sharing around the circle.**

6. *How can children make adults respect their rights?*
   Sharing around the circle.

7. **Warning sign:** *Make a sign* (like in sport games, where they show red or yellow cards), *which you are going to show to the person who does not respect your rights. Think of how that sign could look like, what would be drawn on it... It has to be obvious that it is your sign.*
   When they finish the drawing:
   Sharing around the circle: *Show and describe your sign.*

8. **Closing game: Kiss.** They all stand in a circle. One child walks around the inside of the circle until the leader says: "Stop!" The person in front of whom the child has stopped goes with him to the middle of the circle. There they stand facing each other. The other children count to three. At "three" both players in the center of the circle turn their heads in the direction they choose, either left or right. If they turned their heads in the same direction, they have to kiss each other. If not, they raise their hands and clap them (left hand of one player claps the right hand of the other, and the other way around). Then the second child stays inside the circle and walks around. The game continues until all the children have been in the middle of the circle.

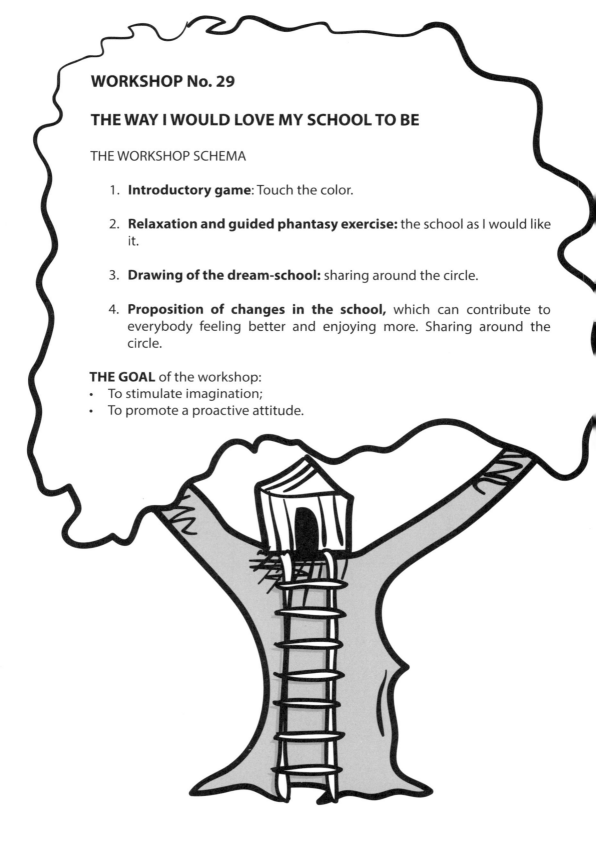

WORKSHOP No. 29

THE WAY I WOULD LOVE MY SCHOOL TO BE

THE WORKSHOP SCHEMA

1. **Introductory game**: Touch the color.

2. **Relaxation and guided phantasy exercise:** the school as I would like it.

3. **Drawing of the dream-school:** sharing around the circle.

4. **Proposition of changes in the school,** which can contribute to everybody feeling better and enjoying more. Sharing around the circle.

THE GOAL of the workshop:
- To stimulate imagination;
- To promote a proactive attitude.

THE WAY I WOULD LOVE MY SCHOOL TO BE

1. **Introductory game: Touch the color.** When WL names a color, every child is supposed to touch some peace of cloth in that color on the other children.

2. **Relaxation and guided phantasy exercise: school as I would like it**
   Before the exercise WL shortly explains to children:
   • they need to keep their eyes closed during the whole exercise;
   • They will participate in a relaxation and guided phantasy exercise.

   After the children find a comfortable position, WL starts to speak slowly, pausing often at the appropriate places in order to give the children time for the experience.

   a. Relaxation: *Breathe rhythmically, relax your legs and hands, feel that your head is relaxed, and your neck, and slowly try to find the most comfortable position. Close your eyes. I will take you to an imaginary journey. Now take several very deep breaths. OK. Your eyes are closed and while I am talking you imagine that you go towards a very lovely place... Pause.*

   b. Guided fantasy: *Imagine that you can create the school just as you would like it. Imagine how it would look like. Imagine the building of the school, how it would look like. Pause. Imagine your classroom, what is inside of it? Imagine who is teaching you. How the school schedule looks like, how long one unit takes. Imagine what you are doing in your dream-school. What does the break look like? Imagine the school yard. What do you see there? Imagine everything you would like in that school of your dreams...*

3. **Drawing the dreamed-school**: *now present with lines, forms, colors where you were, what the school looks like, how you felt, what did you see and experience.*
Put your experience on the paper. It is not so important how well you draw, it is important that you know what the drawing means to you.
After they finish drawing:
Sharing around the circle: what does your dreamed-school look like?

4. **The way I would like my school to be: Proposition of changes in the school**, which can contribute to everybody feeling better and more joyful.
Sharing around the circle.

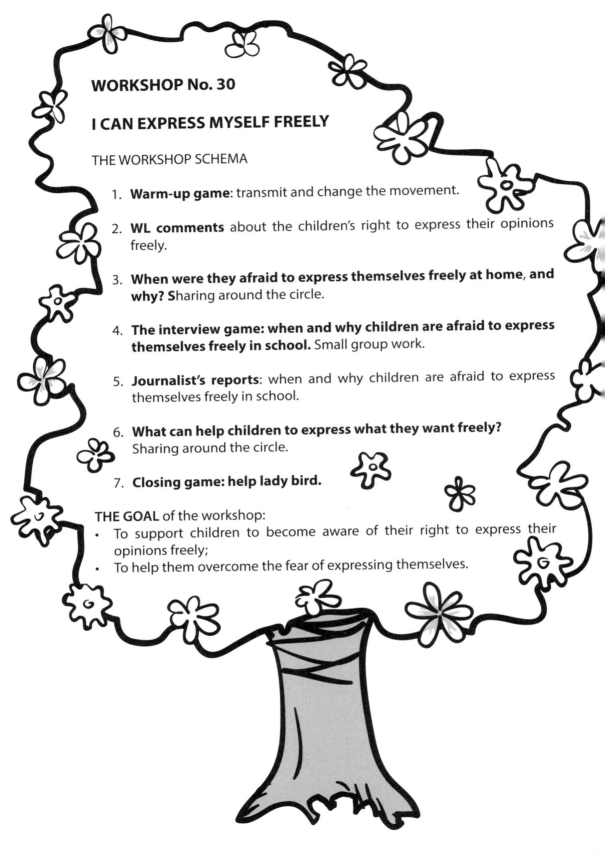

WORKSHOP No. 30

I CAN EXPRESS MYSELF FREELY

THE WORKSHOP SCHEMA

1. **Warm-up game**: transmit and change the movement.

2. **WL comments** about the children's right to express their opinions freely.

3. **When were they afraid to express themselves freely at home, and why? S**haring around the circle.

4. **The interview game: when and why children are afraid to express themselves freely in school.** Small group work.

5. **Journalist's reports**: when and why children are afraid to express themselves freely in school.

6. **What can help children to express what they want freely?** Sharing around the circle.

7. **Closing game: help lady bird.**

THE GOAL of the workshop:
- To support children to become aware of their right to express their opinions freely;
- To help them overcome the fear of expressing themselves.

WORKSHOP No. 30

I CAN EXPRESS MYSELF FREELY

1. **Warming-up game: transmit and change the movement.**
   Everybody stands in a circle. WL makes some unusual movement and transmits it to the child standing next to him, the next child repeats it, adds something of his own and transmits it to the next child, and so on.

2. **WL gives information** about the children's right to express their own opinion freely and that adults are supposed to listen to them when they are making decisions concerning children (Convention on children rights, point 12)

3. **When were they afraid to express themselves freely at home, and why?** Sharing around the circle.

4. **The interview game: when and why children are afraid to express themselves freely in school.** Children are in small groups of 4-5. One member of the group is playing a journalist interviewing the others about when and why children are afraid to express themselves freely in school.

5. **Journalists reports**: when and why children are afraid to express themselves freely in the school.

6. **What can help children to express what they want freely?**
   Sharing around the circle.

7. **Closing game: help lady bird to travel safely.**
   WL is holding an imaginary lady bird between his palms and gives it to the child next to him; the child is receiving it quickly and gently between his palms and gives it to the next child. Everybody is free to do it in his own way.

WORKSHOP No. 31

EVALUATION: CHANGES WITHIN ME

THE WORKSHOP SCHEMA

1. **Evaluation of the workshops**: responding to the 3 questions.

2. **Evaluation of the changes within them**. Drawing of changes in them. Sharing around the circle.

3. **Evaluation of the changes** between them.

EVALUATION: CHANGES WITHIN ME

1. **Evaluation of the workshops: responding to the questions.**
   WL is briefly informing the children that this activity serves to assess the entire workshop-program.
   The children are invited to reflect about 3 questions in regards to all the signs at the panel from all the workshops they passed. (At the end of each workshop WL is supposed to, together with the children, make symbol/ drawings for that workshop and put it up on a panel).
   Children are sharing around the circle and WL writes down their answers:
   1. What was pleasant for them in the workshops? What elements did they enjoy the most? Why?
   2. Was there anything they did not like? What was it? Why did they not like it?
   3. Choose your favorite workshop.

2. **Evaluation of the changes within them.**
   WL invites them to look within themselves for what has changed for them? How can they present this in a drawing, using colors, forms, lines and symbols? What was it like before, and how is it now?
   Every child is drawing himself/herself before and after the program of the workshops.
   After they finish drawing, WL asks them to give their drawings a name. Encourage children to use their imagination, and inform them that it is important to express what is true for them, no matter if something changed or not.
   Sharing around the circle.

3. **Evaluation of the changes between them.**
   WL invites them to look if anything has changed between them, in the group.
   Sharing around the circle.

WORKSHOP No. 32

PRESENTING THE RESULTS OF THE PROGRAM TO THE PARENTS

WL and children together prepare an exhibition of the children's creations, a presentation of the program, and the evaluation results.

THE WORKSHOP SCHEMA

At the meeting with the parents:
1. **Exhibition**
2. **Presentation of the program and evaluation results**
3. **Parents comments**
4. **Children are teaching parents some of their favorite games from the program**
5. **Exchange of positive messages:**
   Parents write and give to their child: what I like about my child.
   Children write and give to their parents: what I like about my mom, dad...
   Sharing in the group (whoever wants to speak): how are they feeling now?

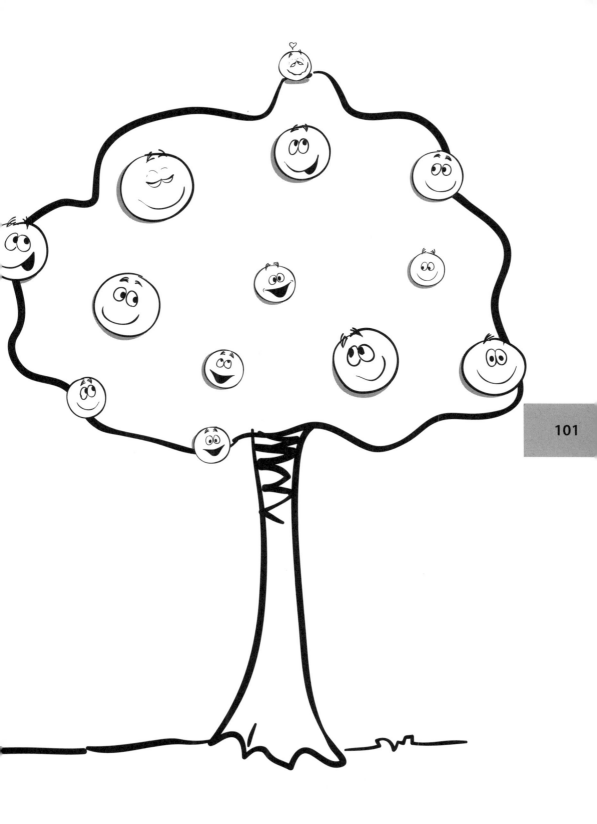

REVIEW

The 'Smile Keepers' program has been specifically developed for children and those adults who interact with children on a daily basis. It actively involves children in a series of stimulating activities, which promote changes in their lives.

The workshops are based on the interactionistic theory of psychic growth (e.g. theory where social interaction is the basic constructive agent of a child's development). These workshops effectively integrate techniques for relaxation, self-expression, and self-control building (based on biofeedback theory and various modern psychotherapies), as well as interactive techniques (derived from social interaction and social feedback theories). The essence of the program transmits through the sequence of the specifically designed interactive workshops. In other words, the main content and the main value of the program lies in the originality of the workshops (even though they were derived from biofeedback theory or social interaction theory) and in the originality of the whole composition of the workshops-sequence. In this very system the child is in the center of the program, and its psychologically stimulating activities. This way:

a) a child can 'open his/her heart' in a physically and emotionally relaxed atmosphere e.g. externalize inner experiences;

b) in the process of this externalization (verbal statements, drawings, scenes played out, etc.) the phenomena of catharsis and simple feedback, i.e. insight in what was externalized takes place;

c) externalization of individual experiences lead to the insight that similar experiences (e.g. fear, anger, etc.) do happen to others too, and generate insights concerning similarities and differences between other members of the social group;

d) children are asked to verbalize their own, as well as the experiences of others which helps them to learn about themselves; (e.g. to get explicit knowledge of what is going on inside of them);

e) in interactive workshops (i.e. those on sources of misunderstandings, social conflicts, nonverbal communication, etc.) social feedback is asked for, namely, how others respond to one's behavior and personal experiences, and there is a search for mutual solutions of mutual problems, so they can see themselves in relation to others and learn various psychological skills (techniques) for solving interpersonal problems, i.e. mutual constructions are developed;

f) Adults - workshop leaders have a discrete, but very important supportive role: to monitor the whole process of the children's development over the course of the workshop series: to discreetly organize workshop settings, to be special partners, all together assuring the success of the developmental process. In this system of workshops a child is an active participant, learning through experience, acquiring knowledge, techniques and skills, which will help to deal with difficult life events and coping problems. This experiential, educative system is especially beneficial in relation to the needs of children affected by war (refugees, children who suffered great losses, who experienced intensive fear or, more general: children under post-traumatic stress syndrome). And it should be pointed out that the program is also beneficial for children who live in our country today, where life is stressful in many aspects, because of the recent war, the destruction and poverty. In and of itself, the program would be a useful innovation in education, also in less dramatic, normal developmental environments, because of the active participation of the children, which is something that is to a large extent lacking in our educational system.

To realize all the intended and possible effects of the program it is necessary:
a) To educate workshop leaders in the workshop system;
b) to experientially determine the optimal number of children in each group; during the fist phase of realization;
c) to empirically monitor, if verbal instructions and requests are in tune with the developmental stages of the children;
d) while leading workshops: to feel at liberty to make changes in accordance with each individual group, the children's responses, and degree to which they are getting involved;
e) To evaluate at least the first effects of the program (do adults notice some changes in children who attended the program, how do children themselves view the benefits, are there any signs that the children apply some things from the program in the other contexts.
In closing, this program, and its many possibilities of application will hopefully attract a lot of support, because it is an important innovation in education, and could be really effective for children affected by war and for children in general.

Prof. Dr. Ivan Ivić
Developmental Psychology professor at Faculty of Philosophy in Belgrade
Belgrade, July 15th 1993.

A SHORT BIOGRAPHY OF NADA IGNJATOVIĆ-SAVIĆ

Born in 1947, **Nada Ignjatović-Savić** has been teaching and carrying out research in developmental psychology at the University of Belgrade for more than 30 years. She has conducted many research and intervention projects, and published several books and programs in the field of personal development, communication, social interaction and education.

Co-founder of the Center for non-violent communication "Smile Keepers", a non-governmental organization focusing primarily on human development, self and group awareness raising, reconstruction of educational practice and social change, Mrs. Nada Ignjatović-Savić was also its executive director.

From 1993 – 2001 she was the director of several intervention projects in education supported by UNICEF, EU, Norwegian People Aid, and Save the Children Trust. During this period she also offered different programs of education for peace and healing the wounds of the war with many groups from former Yugoslavia. During the period between 2000 - 2002 she was a member of the program committee and trainer in two international peace projects - "Olympic Games for Children" (participants were children and professionals from 10 countries) held in Delphi and Olympia, Greece, and "The Day After- Peace and Reconciliation Work with Israeli and Palestinian Religious Leaders, Business, University and Media People", held in Rome and Jerusalem.

Since 1993 when certified by Marshall Rosenberg as a trainer of Nonviolent Communication (NVC), she has been a co-trainer with him of many ten-day intensive international trainings, and has been very active in offering NVC trainings in European countries, Israel and India.

In 2003 in Pilion, Greece she taught NVC to the team of the project: "Human Rights and Conflict Management" organized by the European Network of Women, with the support of EU and Greek General Secretariat for Youth.

She is Coordinator for Serbia of the Earth Stewards Network, an international network of people dedicated to peace, global communication, conflict resolution, citizen diplomacy founded 1979 by the psychologist Danaan Parry. Since 1996 she is an accredited EP facilitator (Essential Peacemaking/ Women & Men). With Chris Gardner she offered EP training to many groups of men and women from different countries in Ex-Yugoslavia and Europe.

In the period 2001 – 2004 she was engaged by the Ministry of Education of Serbia and was a member of the team of experts assigned to develop democratization in education and reform of the school system. She is the author of the programs of Civic Education for Elementary School Children.

Nada Ignjatović-Savić passed away on July 19, 2011 in Belgrade.

SELECTED LIST OF PUBLICATIONS

• Ignjatović-Savić N., Kovač-Cerović T., Plut D., Pešikan A.: **Social Interaction and its developmental effects** in Valsiner J. (Ed): "Child Development within culturally structured environments", Ablex, 1988, 89-159;

• Ignjatović-Savić N.: **Le developpement de la cognition sociale chez les enfants prescolaires: une approche interactive**, in "Quelles recherches, quelles demarches pour que tous les enfants developpent leurs potentialites?", CRESAS-INRP, Paris, 1992;

• Ignjatović-Savić N.: **Expecting the unexpected; A view on child development from war affected social context,** in Psihologija, Journal of the Serbian Psychological Association, Vol.XXVIII, Special Issue 1995.

PROGRAMS AND MANUALS

• **"Smile keepers"** (two training programs for psychologists and teachers aiming to develop their personal and professional competence), 1993;

• 3 manuals **Smile keepers I, II, and III** - with programs for children aged 5-10, 11-15, and 15-18, published by the Institute of Psychology in Belgrade, 1994. The content of the programs is designed to help children to develop strategies to cope with emotional experience (fears, sadness, grief, anger), conflicts and to develop self and social awareness;

• "Mutual **education**", training program in nonviolent communication for professionals working with children, 1995;

• Co-author of the three manuals for teachers **"Words are windows or they are walls 1, 2 and 3"** offering nonviolent communication programs for children aged 5-10, 11-14, 15-18. Published by Institute of psychology, 1996. The manuals are translated to German, English, Polish, Danish and Italian, and used in many kindergartens and schools in Europe;

• **"Civic education 1 and 2 and 3"**- programs of civic education for the first, second and third grade of elementary school, published by the Ministry of education of Serbia, 2002-2004.

TABLE OF CONTENTS

OTHER BOOKS AVAILABLE IN ENGLISH:

Smile keepers 2 - program for promoting self and social awareness development psychological workshops for children 11-14 years of age. The content of the program is designed to help children to develop strategies to cope with emotional experience (fears, sadness, grief, anger), conflicts and to develop self and social awareness; contact: *book@krnvc.org*.

"SMILE KEEPERS" EDITIONS IN OTHER LANGUAGES:

• **Smile Keepers 1, 2 and 3** in Serbian (1993, 1995, 1997);
contact: *cncsmilekeepers@gmail.com*

• **Smile Keepers 1 and 2**

- in Polish (2009), under the title "Strażnicy uśmiechu 1 & 2"

- in German (volume1, 2015), under the title "Smile Keepers, Bd. 1: Hüter des Lächelns"; volume 2 to be published; contact: *www.synergia-verlag.ch*

- in Korean (2013); contact: *book@krnvc.org*

- in French (2017); contact: *sg@girasol.be*

- in English (2018); contact: *book@krnvc.org*

- in Chinese, to be published; contact: *book@krnvc.org*

CONTACT INFORMATION:

The Korean Center for Nonviolent Communication
3F. Namyang BLDG. 23, Samseong-ro 95-gil,
Gangnam-gu, Seoul, South Korea

e-mail: book@krnvc.org